British History in Perspective
General Editor: Jeremy Black

PUBLISHED TITLES

Peter Catterall *The Labour Party, 1918–1945*
Gregory Claeys *The French Revolution Debate in Britain*
Pauline Croft *James I*
Eveline Cruickshanks *The Glorious Revolution*
John Davis *British Politics, 1885–1939*
David Dean *Parliament and Politics in Elizabethan and Jacobean England, 1558–1614*
Susan Doran *English Foreign Policy in the Sixteenth Century*
David Eastwood *England, 1750–1850: Government and Community in the Provinces*
Colin Eldridge *The Victorians Overseas*
Richard English *The IRA*
Angus Hawkins *British Party Politics, 1852–1886*
H. S. Jones *Political Thought in Nineteenth-Century Britain*
D. E. Kennedy *The English Revolution, 1642–1649*
Carol Levin *The Reign of Elizabeth I*
W. David McIntyre *British Decolonisation*
A. P. Martinich *Thomas Hobbes*
R. C. Nash *English Foreign Trade and the World Economy, 1600–1800*
Richard Ovendale *Anglo-American Relations in the Twentieth Century*
Ian Packer *Lloyd George*
Murray Pittock *Cultural Identities in Britain and Ireland, 1685–1789*
Murray Pittock *Jacobitism*
David Powell *The Edwardian Crisis: Britain, 1901–1914*
Robin Prior and Trevor Wilson *Britain and the Impact of World War I*
Brian Quintrell *Government and Politics in Early Stuart England*
Philip Riden *The Industrial Revolution*
Stephen Roberts *Governance in England and Wales, 1603–1688*
David Scott *The British Civil Wars*
John Spellman *John Locke*
W. Stafford *John Stuart Mill*
Alan Sykes *The Radical Right in Britain*
Ann Weikel *The Elizabethan Counter-Reformation*
Ann Williams *Kingship and Government in Pre-Conquest England*
Ian Wood *Churchill*
Michael Young *Charles I*

History of Ireland

Toby Barnard *The Kingdom of Ireland, 1641–1740*
Sean Duffy *Ireland in the Middle Ages*
Alan Heesom *The Anglo-Irish Union, 1800–1922*
Hiram Morgan *Ireland in the Early Modern Periphery, 1534–1690*

History of Scotland

I. G. C. Hutchison *Scottish Politics in the Twentieth Century*
Roger Mason *Kingship and Tyranny? Scotland, 1513–1603*
John McCaffrey *Scotland in the Nineteenth Century*
John Shaw *The Political History of Eighteenth-Century Scotland*
Bruce Webster *Medieval Scotland*

History of Wales

Gareth Jones *Wales, 1700–1980: Crisis of Identity*

Please note that a sister series, *Social History in Perspective*, is now available. It covers the key topics in social, cultural and religious history.

PARTY AND POLITICS, 1830–1852

ROBERT STEWART

First published 1989 by
MACMILLAN PRESS LTD
Houndmills, Basingstoke, Hampshire RG21 6XS
and London
Companies and representatives
throughout the world

ISBN 0–333–43626–1

A catalogue record for this book is available
from the British Library.

9   8   7   6   5   4   3   2
03   02   01   00   99   98   97   96

Printed in Hong Kong

CONTENTS

v

1

THE OLD ORDER

It is the peculiar happiness of these our days that the distinctions of
Whig and Tory are either so little known or so totally confounded
by the practice of both the parties that it is no easy task to define
either, but, as it has been the wicked policy of some who wish to
disturb the public peace to endeavour to revive those odious and
obsolete distinctions, a short history of both may be useful by way
of antidote and to show how little they have to do with the contests
for power in these our days.

Those words, written in about 1760 by the Oxfordshire squire
and member of parliament, Sir Roger Newdigate,[1] expressed
neatly the status of party in Great Britain at the accession of
George III. Party was nearly extinct and nearly universally
execrated. The crown was the pivot on which political life turned.
Every government in Hanoverian England, in fact as well as
in name, was the king's government. Ministers derived their
authority from the crown and were responsible for their actions
to the monarch, whose disfavour signalled their demise. Seventy
years after Sir Roger was writing, the crown had ceased to be
the single most important element in the political arena. Since
1832 every government has derived its authority from parliament
and depended for its existence upon parliamentary favour. And
since parliaments have been, since 1832, divided into parties,
the change was, in effect, from royal government to party
government. That change did not take place overnight. Its
origins lay as far back as the 17th-century quarrels between
Charles I and his parliamentary opponents; its formative years

1

were the closing decades of the 18th century. The change amounted to this, that the executive (or government), which had previously acknowledged parliament's rudimentary power to scrutinise and, in exceptional circumstances, check its actions, came gradually to accept that parliament (and hence, as it turned out, party) was the instrument by which it was enabled to act at all. Government *limited by* parliament gave way to government *carried on through* parliament. As the crown withdrew at an *andante* pace from active politics, party grew into an institution capable of replacing it as the foundation of governments.

The gradual decline of the crown's political authority, a process assisted by the whittling away of its sources of patronage,[2] was more a symptom than a cause of the rise of party. The causes lay deeper, in the jolt which the French Revolution gave to Englishmen's perceptions and, deeper still, in the disruptive social and economic changes which, in addition to providing part of the context of men's reactions to events in France, induced them to ponder the scope of government responsibility for the well-being of the country and to ask themselves what number and which sorts of people ought to have a voice in the affairs of government. By 1830 the division, blurred though it was, between those who thought that both the narrow range of the executive's duties and the tiny size of the 'political nation' were inadequate to provide stable and effective government in a society whose industry, towns and population were all growing at a startling pace and those who resisted their arguments had come to be the central division in politics. That division was reflected in the hardening of party allegiances. And, even though the broadening of government activity in the 1820s, the foundation of the early Victorian 'revolution in government', was the work of Tory cabinets, the division lay, broadly speaking, between a progressive, forward-looking Whig Party (with its Radical hangers-on) and a conservative, defensive Tory Party. By 1830 those two parties had established themselves as the instruments through which political debate was to be conducted and by which governments were to be sustained.[3]

Those parties, Whig and Tory, bore little resemblance to the mass political parties of the 20th century. There was no such thing as party membership gained by the payment of an annual subscription. There were no party conferences. Nor, until late in the 19th century, did anything like party programmes make their appearance. There was scarcely even, when a party was in opposition (as the Whigs were for almost the whole of the period from the fall of the Fox–North coalition in 1783 to the arrival in office of Lord Grey in 1830), such a thing as a party leader. There were simply the opposition leader in the House of Lords and the opposition leader in the House of Commons (the first to be formally chosen by his colleagues was George Tierney in 1818). Although the word 'party' was constantly on the lips of politicians, it took time for men who had grown up believing that a member of parliament's first duty, in normal circumstances, was to support the crown's ministers and that systematic, formed, party opposition was 'factious' and disloyal to accept the legitimacy of party. The very phrase, 'His Majesty's loyal opposition', was first spoken only in 1826, and even then not with the full constitutional weight that it later came to bear.

The object of party, after all, was to combine to gain office and to give effect, once placed there, to certain principles. Party trained its guns on the ancient prerogative rights of the king to choose his ministers and to approve or disapprove their measures. By 1830, though the issue was not quite sealed, those prerogative powers of the crown had virtually disappeared. In 1822 Lord Liverpool, the prime minister, assured George IV that if he resigned all his cabinet colleagues would follow him out of office. In other words, Tory ministers' first loyalty was to the head of the government, not to the crown; and this demise of the crown's authority meant that Liverpool's government was practically, even if not in name, a Tory government. Only in the language of constitutional purists was it the king's government. The transition from royal to party government was neither abrupt nor smooth; nor, understandably, was the fact that it was taking place clearly visible to contemporaries. In 1827 a Whig member of parliament, after observing the defeat of a bill for the relief of Roman Catholics, said that if the crown were favourable to the measure it would pass by more than 70 votes.

Constitutional habits die hard and, since the language in which politics is discussed usually lags behind events, many politicians continued to feel self-conscious when speaking of party. Henry Brougham, the radical-minded Whig who became the lord chancellor in Lord Grey's government, was chastised in 1830 for publishing 'indecent and unconstitutional' details of MPs' votes and party affiliations.[4] In a government publication, *The State of the Nation*, issued in 1822, the word 'Whig' appears only in its historical sense, the word 'Tory' does not appear at all, and the word 'party' is used as a derogatory term for mischief-making faction.[5] Even so, the ease with which many politicians spoke of party is striking, as is the assumption implicit in their language that party had become an essential feature of the constitution. William Gladstone wrote in 1841 that the 'principle of party' had 'long predominated in this country' and in 1830 John Croker, a long-serving member of parliament and the chief contributor of political essays to the Tory *Quarterly Review*, gave his opinion that 'party attachments and consistency are in the *first* class of a statesman's duties' and that government by party was 'part of our well-understood, though unwritten, constitution'.[6]

Party organisation, by modern standards, was in its infancy. Survivors of the Pitt and Fox clubs of the 1790s continued, in some places, to carry party feeling into local politics and local electoral organisation was frequently extensive.[7] But no formal relations existed between local election managers and the parties at Westminster, though central funds (too meagre to have any significant national effect) were occasionally made available to a constituency in special circumstances. Elections were, for the most part, local events and at every general election fewer than half, at least, of the seats were contested. Almost all county elections were barren ground for a real contest between parties, since the formidable costs of polling the 40s freeholders over a large area persuaded the opposing sides to share the represen-tation of each county (a county constituency returned either two or three members) between them. In the contemporary jargon that practice was known as preserving 'the peace of the county'. Inside the House of Commons party management was becoming more sophisticated. By the 1820s party leaders had taken over from the Speaker the arrangement of daily business; the whips sent out letters urging members to attend debates and support the party line; the number of meetings of the parliamentary parties rose to one or two every session; and members were more and more instructed how to vote (whether they obeyed the instruction is another question). That degree of organisation was a pointer to the future; in itself it was too weak to enforce party discipline, partly because the central parties, having almost no weight in the constituencies, were unable to bring a delinquent into line by threatening him with the loss of his seat at the next election.[8]

The development of pre-reform parties was of more importance for the future than for the contemporary conduct of government and parliamentary business.

> Party voting [in the House of Commons] did not centre on legislation or even on the salient policies of the government. Instead it sought out issues of general principle in the peripheral areas of government, scandals, cases of maladministration, or questions of reform where public policy was dormant. In the important fields of general legislation, financial policy, trade, the corn laws, commercial and industrial regulations, labour regulations and the poor laws, and all kinds of social questions, the House normally acted through select committees constituted on a non-party basis with little expectation of any party voting when the results came before the House itself. In any session party divisions were few.[9]

The published division lists, which highlight the hardening of party lines in the 1820s, reflected only a small portion of parliament's activity. A host of important legislative measures concerning local trading regulations, the building of harbours, the paving of roads, the establishment of joint-stock companies and the like were introduced by private member's bills and formed a part neither of the government's business nor of the party warfare. And it was legislation of that kind, lying outside the purview of party, that was often of the greatest interest in the constituencies.

There is point to one historian's description of post-Waterloo politics as being characterised by 'the surviving strength of party sentiment and the looseness of party affiliation'.[10] Yet the importance of sentiment is not to be decried. If the nascent state of formal party organisation provides weak ground for the argument that party occupied an important place on the political stage, more compelling evidence presents itself elsewhere: first, in the extent to which the political world had come to be separated *by its attitudes* into Whigs and Tories; second, in the extent to which that distinction was expressed in voting at elections; and, third, in the force that the divide exerted to harden the lines between government and opposition at Westminster and to drive members of parliament who could truly be called 'independents' out of the field.

Since its birth in the late 17th century (during the fierce quarrels which drove James II from the throne) the Whig Party had stood for liberty, in particular the liberty of the subject from executive tyranny and religious oppression. The Whigs' notions of liberty were never very broad. They did not inquire into the meaning that liberty might have for the overwhelming proportion of the people who owned no property. Liberty in the 17th century was an aristocratic ideal: it meant wresting specific liberties, or privileges, from the crown. It meant being left to pursue a private life and a career in business without, as the great 18th-century apologist for the established order, Bishop Paley, put it, 'inspection, scrutiny, and control'. The ends to which the Whigs invoked the name of liberty were the sanctity of private property and the ordering of society into a more or less permanent hierarchy. On that fundamental ground there was no disagreement between Whigs and Tories, and for so long as no great issue arose to ruffle the complacency of the landed class, the division within it into Whig and Tory faded into insignificance. So it was for most of the 18th century, which, as one historian has written, 'lacked the fundamental conflicts of its predecessor, and without great issues parties are always slow to crystallize'.[11]

Still, the tradition survived that, as the Whig member of parliament, Sir James Mackintosh, was pleased to point out, 'a Tory is more influenced by loyalty, and a Whig by the love of liberty',[12] and the bare bones of that tradition gained new flesh when the American War of Independence, the French

Revolution, the Radicals' agitation for parliamentary reform, the Nonconformists' campaign for civil liberties and the machine-breaking protests of the Luddites and others introduced a new question into English politics. That question was whether the greater threat to liberty came from the crown and the executive or from popular agitation and unrest. At its simplest, the Whig answer was that it came from the crown, the Tory answer that it came from the 'mob'. So the Whig response to popular demands tended towards accommodation, the Tory towards repression.

For a time the Tories had the better of the argument. The 'patriotic' rallying to the crown and its ministers during the long wars against Napoleonic France stifled reformist activity and enfeebled the small Whig Party in parliament. But after the return to peace in 1815 and the economic distress which the winding-down of a war-boosted economy entailed, radicalism was once again loud in the land and issues such as free trade *versus* the corn laws, electoral reform *versus* constitutional rigidity and religious equality *versus* Anglican monopoly gathered urgency. As they did so it became more and more difficult for members of parliament to behave independently of party and to declare themselves simply as supporters of 'the king's government'. They were more and more drawn into giving a consistent support to the actions and policies of the Tory government or to the projects of the Whig opposition. In 1804 Charles James Fox put the number of independents in the House of Commons at 180; by 1831 the number had fallen to the 15 'moderates' who voted for the reform bill on its second reading, but who displayed their 'independence' by voting also, a few weeks later, for a Tory wrecking amendment in committee.

In the 1820s attendance at debates became more regular – the number of members who failed to turn up for a whole session fell from more than 200 in Pitt's time to barely 100 in Lord Liverpool's – and voting followed a more consistent party pattern. By the latter years of Liverpool's prime ministership at least five-sixths of the House of Commons consisted of members who, if not avowed party men, behaved in the division lobbies as if they were,[13] so that the House had come to operate within 'a two-party system modified by the existence of unreliable groups on the fringes of both sides'.[14] It is true that in 1827 the relative stability of parties was disrupted when George Canning formed his government: the bulk of the Tories refused to support him and he was forced to enter into coalition with some of the Whigs. But far from revealing the weakness of party, the episode disclosed how deeply party had become engrained in English politics. The Tories who deserted Canning also, by refusing to lend their support to the king's chosen ministers, deserted the crown. They put political, and to a large degree party, considerations – hostility to Canning and opposition to Roman Catholic relief – above their duty to the sovereign. And those Whigs who came to Canning's rescue were denounced by Lord Grey and his political friends for betraying the Whig Party. Everywhere voices were heard lamenting the break-up of parties; in a non-party system their laments would have been impossible.

Beyond Westminster, too, in the country at large, there were signs of the increasing influence of party. Bribery and corruption, rotten boroughs and the high incidence of uncontested elections did not altogether defeat the play of opinion at the polls. Recent investigation of pre-reform elections has led one historian to conclude that 'everything points to a substantial resurgence of popular political participation after 1761' and, after discovering that most voters in two-member and three-member constituencies 'plumped' for candidates of the same side, that voting was 'a carefully considered as well as a carefully controlled activity and one which operated within a party framework'.[15] These are controversial statements and the arguments surrounding them are complex, but they accord with the revival of the names 'Whig' and 'Tory' at the elections of 1807. The clearest evidence of the alignment of parties according to issues at elections comes from the Dissenters, whose votes, together with those of commercial and industrial interests, made the Whigs more successful in the large boroughs than the Tories. In the more populous counties, too, where the 40s freeholders were strong enough to overcome the influence of the great landowners, the opposition had more MPs than the government. The Whigs, Austin Mitchell has written, had 'a clear claim to be the most popular party',[16] though it might be more accurate to speak in this way of 'the opposition', since many of the populous boroughs returned Radicals who cannot be strictly numbered among the Whigs.

Further development of parties was unnecessary so long as the 'political nation', that section of the population involved in political decision-making at some level, remained tiny and representative of one class almost exclusively, the landed aristocracy and gentry. The House of Commons was remarkable for its inbreeding. When, for instance, 113 MPs signed a requisition inviting George Tierney to lead the Whigs in the lower House in 1818, at least 51 of them were related to one another.[17] Lords and Commons were knit together by close family ties. One-quarter of the House of Commons consisted of sons of peers and in 1827 Croker, in order to demonstrate 'how impossible it is to do anything satisfactory towards [forming] a Government in this country without the help of the aristocracy', sent Canning lists showing that the Tory peers alone controlled the election of 207 members of the House of Commons and the Whigs 73 more.[18] So narrow a governing elite, with few electors to satisfy, was able to discuss matters of public policy at country houses and secure votes in the division lobbies by patronage, family connection and ancestral friendships. On the eve of the reform bill the electorate in England and Wales, though precise figures are unavailable, amounted to about 325,000, or little more than 3 per cent of the population. The figure for Scotland was much lower still, at about 3,500. The landed elite, defined as those members of the aristocracy and gentry with an annual income of more than £1,000, consisted of about 4,000 families. (The 'New Domesday' survey of landownership in 1873 revealed that about 7,000 families owned 80 per cent of the nation's land.) That elite not only controlled elections and filled the parliamentary benches – a statute of 1710 which created a *landed* property qualification for members of parliament (£600 for county representatives, £300 for borough) was passed to exclude rich 'strangers' such as brewers and bankers from parliament – it also supplied the officers in the armed services, the senior officials in the diplomatic service, the clergy of the established Church and the higher luminaries of the judiciary. Locally, too, through their service as lords-lieutenant of the counties and magistrates at petty and quarter sessions, they governed the ordinary lives of the people. The land had a powerful partner in the Church. It collected tithes and Church rates, from Dissenters as well as its own communicants; it had a monopoly of higher education, at Oxford and Cambridge, England's only universities (undergraduates were required to subscribe to the Thirty-Nine Articles of the Church of England; no religious test was applied to undergraduates at Scottish universities); its bishops sat in the House of Lords; its clergy supplied one-quarter of the justices of the peace; and by its influence in the local parish vestries it had a large voice in matters such as the operation of parish relief for the poor and the setting of the parish rate.

The Church retained its authority even while its actual hold over the minds of people was being steadily undermined by the growth of the Dissenting sects. By 1815 there were more Dissenters' chapels than Anglican churches in the towns of England and Wales, though Anglicanism kept its lead in the country as a whole until mid-century. Similarly, though the land remained the largest 'interest' in the state, agriculture no longer dominated the economy as it continued to do in the rest of Europe. Between 1784 and 1830 the value of manufacturing exports quadrupled; by then agriculture was providing less than one-third of the national income. Yet the law stood that however much real property a man left at his death, his creditors received nothing unless he also left personal property and, another instance of the political power of the landed class, that if a man borrowed money and applied it to the cultivation of land, his creditors had no redress if he died before making repayment.

In parliament the landed interest did not have exclusive sway. The commercial interest was represented in the House of Commons in the 1820s by about 100 members, chief among them bankers, financiers and the great merchants, especially, among the last, the East and West Indian traders. The bulk of the nation, however, consisting of the lower and middling orders, was excluded. The pre-reform franchise was so irregular that there were places where artisans did, it is true, have the vote:

framework-knitters formed the largest occupational group in Nottingham's electorate, for example, and Nottingham, though exceptional, was not unique. Even so, parliament was a body of the rich, elected by the rich and speaking for the rich. The infamous corn law of 1815, which placed so high a tariff on the import of foreign wheat that it was almost impossible for foreign grain to enter the country, was passed partly, no doubt, to maintain domestic food-production against the possibility of renewed war with France, but also in order to keep up bread prices at inflated wartime levels for the benefit of the owners of agricultural estates. At the same time the repeal of the property and income tax in 1816, hailed by the Whigs as a great popular victory over the Tory government, eased the burden of direct taxation on landowners and increased the responsibility of consumers to supply the government's revenue by indirect taxation.

The 'political nation' was no doubt somewhat larger than the electorate. In his *Letters on a Regicide Peace*, published in 1796, Edmund Burke defined what that nation was and made an estimate of its size.

> Those who, in any *political* view, are to be called the people are of adult age, not declining in life, of tolerable leisure for such discussions, and of some means of information, above menial dependence; i.e. about 400,000. This is the British public; and it is a public very numerous. The rest, when feeble, are the objects of protection; when strong, the means of force.[19]

Burke's estimate was probably slightly under the mark. A rough-and-ready method of measuring the political nation is to compare the signatures on petitions to parliament on matters of public policy with the names listed on the electoral registers. Such comparisons yield two conclusions. First, the unfranchised members of the public who demonstrated their interest in politics by signing petitions held firm views which disclosed a consistent political stance (as did the voters themselves, whose opinions as expressed in petitions closely coincided with their opinions as expressed at parliamentary elections); for a great number of people the signing of a petition was not a capricious act. Second, the political nation, enumerated in this way, was, at 500,000 or so, about double the size of the electorate, or about 25 per cent of the adult male population.[20] (It was that disparity between the number of people able to vote and the number of them who demonstrated, to use contemporary language and standards of judgement, their 'fitness' to do so which lent, eventually, irresistible strength to the demand for an extension of the franchise.)

That wider public opinion exercised mounting pressure on parliament and the executive as time passed. In the first five years of the younger Pitt's administration, ending in 1789, 880 petitions were presented to the House of Commons; the number grew steadily until, in the five years from 1826 to 1831, it reached nearly 25,000.[21] In times of crisis that pressure was decisive. Two famous victories for 'the people' against the House of Commons were won in the 1770s, each the result of the 'Wilkes and liberty' commotion: the right to publish parliamentary debates and the right of an elected member of parliament not to be arbitrarily declared by the House of Commons to be ineligible to take his seat. Both the repeal of the Orders-in-Council (Great Britain's response, in the trade war with France, to Napoleon's continental blockade) in 1812 and the repeal of the property and income tax four years later were the fruit of carefully mounted, mass petitioning campaigns.

Despite occasional reverses, however, the landed interest was so ascendant that some historians have spoken of a classless Hanoverian society. Such language accords with the perceptions of the Hanoverian oligarchy itself, which believed (or professed to believe) that society was divided vertically into 'interests' (that is, not horizontally, as in a class model, by income, occupation, etc.), so that the great landowner spoke for, and in parliament 'virtually represented', the agricultural labourer, the butcher, the blacksmith, all those persons whose lives were encompassed by the agricultural economy and whose social positions were defined within the hierarchy of the rural 'family'. Similarly, although the argument became more difficult to sustain when it was applied to urban society, the great merchants and manufacturers were said to 'represent' the artisans and shopkeepers beneath them.

The political and social theory of the old order was inhabited by 'gentlemen', 'people' and the 'mob', vocabulary heavy in moral nuance. The 'people' – men of property below the gentry, including yeomen, freeholders, merchants, manufacturers and members of the learned professions – were on the periphery of the ruling circle, their claim to a voice in the political process partially recognised. The 'mob' was excluded. By the early decades of the 19th century that language was beginning to be replaced by the language of class,[22] language which gave expression to the tensions and conflicts *within* the old 'interests' and which suggested that men in different walks of life but of similar economic and social status had common grievances which could be redressed by common action. The extent to which either the working classes or the middling classes had developed a class-consciousness by 1830 is the subject of lively debate among historians. E. P. Thompson's argument that the most important fact of the period between 1790 and 1830 was the development of working-class identity and organisation, so that by the end of the period the working-class presence was the most important element in English political life, has had a cool reception.[23] (Since, indeed, working-class men filled scarcely any office of authority, local or national, nor exhibited any power to direct the decisions of the men who did, Professor Thompson, though writing as an historian, means actually that it *ought* to have been the most important element.) So has his argument that a working-class revolution failed in those years only because of a strenuous counter-revolutionary stand by the governing class and the restraining, conservative influence of Methodism on the common people.[24] Yet there is no denying that the ruling classes, their antipathy to change and their fear of radicalism stiffened by their experience of the French Revolution, did their best to strangle working men's ambitions. They placed a stamp duty on newspapers – 'taxes on knowledge' as they came to be called – to put information beyond the range of the poor; they upheld stringent libel laws to stifle public debate; they suppressed associations for the reform of parliament; and they outlawed workers' combinations (early trade unions) to improve wages and the conditions of work. Most important of all, perhaps, they denied that the grievances of the poor – starvation wages, insecurity of employment, high food prices – were the stuff of politics. Year after year (though some of their actions, like the 1815 corn law, belied their statements) government ministers instructed the nation in the incompetence of parliament and the law to influence the course of economic affairs or to relieve the hardships of the people.

The public challenge to the intentions of the ruling classes gained strength as the 19th century progressed and as the 'moral economy' of an earlier, socially more homogeneous, generation dissolved in the new urban, industrial acid – in 1814 parliament stripped magistrates of the power to fix wages in their localities at a 'just' level – and principles of the free operation of the market gained ground. The working class, organising itself in underground trade combinations and reading the radical propaganda prepared for it in the unstamped press, came more and more to be persuaded that spasmodic violence – the old methods of 'collective bargaining by riot' and machine-breaking – was a feeble weapon in the class war. Workers listened to men like William Cobbett, who travelled around the country instructing them that the true cause of the suffering was mis-government and that deliverance from hardship and injustice lay in the reform of parliament. Whether it makes sense to speak of working-class consciousness or class identity, it is certain that great numbers of skilled and unskilled labourers were becoming politically radical. In 1817 Robert Southey, the poet and Tory political theorist, warned Lord Liverpool that Jacobinism (a word, borrowed from the French, for political extremism) had spread beyond the middle classes and 'sunk into the rabble';[25] three years later Lord Grey had come to the opinion that 'nine-tenths of the lower and middling ranks' were 'eagerly bent' on reform.[26]

The middling ranks presented the more potent and the more immediate challenge to the ascendancy of the landed aristocracy. By 1815 it was becoming a commonplace to speak of the 'people', the non-landed, predominantly urban, trading, manufacturing and professional property-owners, as the backbone of the nation's intellectual and cultural life. The 'middle rank', James Mill wrote in his *Essay on Government* of 1820, gave 'to science, to art, and to legislation itself, their most distinguished ornaments'.[27] Yet small businessmen and shopkeepers and the new industrialists, especially the cotton masters in the north, remained for the most part unfranchised. The growth of Dissent, too, was largely unrecognised officially. Middle-class Dissent was the nursery of pre-reform radicalism, not only because the demands of the Dissenters for political and civil equality had not been answered, but also because Dissent, although it was not an exclusively urban phenomenon, flourished in those towns where non-landed forms of wealth were rapidly accumulating.

> Large numbers of English people of the business and shop-keeping community ... had become a kind of 'Protestant underworld', a 'second world' outside and beyond the Establishment, if not quite beyond the pale of the Constitution. They had nothing to lose by a remodelling of the institutions in which they had such an exiguous part. They were like the excluded middle-class of France, that natural breeding-ground of *Les Philosophes*, ripe for radical change, though not for revolution.[28]

The French Revolution had introduced notions of natural rights to a large segment of the British population. But the progress of early 19th-century radicalism owed less to abstract theories of justice than it did to the conviction that only a reformation of the electoral system could produce a parliament willing to make the administrative, legal, social and financial reforms which the Radicals were seeking. To both middle-class and working-class Radicals reform was, indeed, a matter of intrinsic justice; but, far more important, it was the first step towards overhauling the structure of the country's institutions. It was not simply the electorate which required expansion; it was the scope of government itself.

2
THE GREAT REFORM ACT

A variety of circumstances brought Lord Grey and the Whigs into office at the end of 1830.[1] One was that the death of George IV in the previous spring had removed the royal ban on the Whigs. William IV was happy to work with them (he was, indeed, to be of signal service in getting the great reform bill on to the statute books). Another was that the elections of 1830, which, as the law then stood, were required by the accession of a new monarch, had revealed a strong current of anti-government sentiment in the most open constituencies and had brought gains to the opposition. Party ties were still too indistinct for a general election to determine the fate of a government at once (the first government to resign immediately after a general election rather than test its strength in parliament was Disraeli's in 1868) and the Duke of Wellington and his ministers remained in office to meet the new parliament. The government ranks were, however, in a sorry state. The Tory Party, held together by Lord Liverpool for fifteen years, had disintegrated into three groups – the Canningites (whom the bulk of the party had refused to act with during Canning's short-lived government in 1827), the regular supporters of Peel and Wellington, and the ultras (estranged from the party leaders by Wellington's decision to turn round on his public statements and preside over the passing of the act of Roman Catholic emancipation). More than half of the government's supporters in the House of Commons had voted against emancipation, and although only a few of them settled

16

into permanent hostility to Wellington's government, the handful who did were sufficient to tip the balance in the Commons when the new parliament assembled in the autumn of 1830. It was their votes, added to those of the Whigs, Radicals and some Canningites, which defeated the Tory government on a minor motion concerning the civil list and persuaded Wellington to resign.

The real cause of the Tories' downfall was Wellington's insensitivity to, or stubbornness in the face of, the evident discontent in the country. After the relatively prosperous years of the mid-1820s, the economy had turned sharply downwards. A slump in manufactures, with the attendant fall in employment and wages, combined with high bread prices to revive memories of the depressed years immediately after Waterloo. The result was not only a resurgence of popular unrest, manifested most acutely in the 'Captain Swing' riots in the south-eastern counties,[2] but a renewed agitation for parliamentary reform, especially in the unrepresented towns of the north like Birmingham, where the banker, Thomas Attwood, formed a Political Union to campaign for electoral reform in December, 1829. Attwood's example was followed in several places and the call for reform was prominent at the 1830 elections, although in a number of constituencies where Dissent was powerful the cry to abolish slavery in the empire was louder. Polling in those days took place over several weeks and in the middle of the elections Denis Le Marchant, secretary to Henry Brougham, whose return for Yorkshire, the most 'open' constituency in the country, was a remarkable triumph for radical Whiggery, reported that 'all parties now seem to admit that public opinion goes against the Duke'.[3] Scotland, with its tiny electorate, was a Tory fief and the rotten boroughs returned a preponderance of ministerialists; but elsewhere, in the 62 'more or less open' constituencies returning 126 members, the *Annual Register* calculated that two-thirds of the successful candidates were in the opposition ranks.[4]

Since the counties made up most of the open constituencies, it appeared that the country gentlemen, an essential source of every Hanoverian ministry's strength in the division lobbies, were drifting away from 'independent' support of the king's government towards opposition. One pamphleteer remarked that 'the combined influence of small properties in the hands of the many' had triumphed over 'the influence of great properties in the hands of the few';[5] another asked whether any prime minister had previously had the county representation so heavily ranged against him.[6] The election results were commonly interpreted as a measure of the willingness of lesser gentlemen and independent farmers to separate themselves from the great landowners and, more widely, as evidence that 'the middle classes are becoming too strong for the aristocracy'.[7] 'Those candidates who stood on the support of Government found no advantage from it', the Duke of Buckingham ruefully concluded, 'but on the contrary were invariably obliged to abandon such ground for the ground of reform and economy, and are committed in almost every instance to conditional engagement on these points.'[8]

Not since Pitt's great victory in 1784 had a general election expressed so clearly the state of opinion in the country. Only a few years earlier Canning had remarked that the nation was 'on the brink of a great struggle between property and population' and that the struggle could be averted only 'by the mildest and most liberal legislation'.[9] Yet Canning, for all his adventurousness in other fields, had been an intransigent opponent of parliamentary reform, and Wellington, too, supported by Peel, had turned his back on the smallest tinkering with the electoral system, even the proposal which came before his cabinet and parliament in 1828 to abolish a couple of notoriously corrupt boroughs and transfer their representation elsewhere. Neither the elections of 1830 nor the unrest in the country (which in places reached an alarming pitch in the autumn) moved the Duke. In one of those parliamentary statements which will live in the memory for as long as English history is recorded, he announced, shortly after the opening of the new parliament, that he 'was fully convinced that the country possessed at the present moment a legislature which answered all the good purposes of legislation' and that 'the legislature and the system of representation possessed the full and entire confidence of the country'.[10] The first part of the statement was debatable; the second was provocative nonsense, a firebrand which ignited the very spirit it was intended to quell.

The Duke later explained, somewhat feebly, that as the king's minister it was his duty to maintain the institutions of the country.[11] More important was his unwillingness, so soon after the shock which Catholic emancipation had given to the Tory Party, to deliver another blow to his supporters by declaring his government's readiness to consider parliamentary reform. Moreover, although hindsight looks upon the years 1831–32 as 'the crisis of reform', Wellington had lived long enough to have seen the sail of reform many times unfurled only to droop in a windless sea.

Whatever his reasons, Wellington's rigidity was his downfall. He not only was forced to surrender the seals of office to Lord Grey, he handed the initiative in politics to the reformers. Reform ceased to be merely one of several contentious issues facing parliament; it became the great dividing line between parties. Between the day that the Whigs came into office and Lord John Russell's introduction of the government's reform bill four months later, only one question mattered: what would the Whigs do?

Lord Grey's cabinet, one of the most aristocratic of the century and probably the richest,[12] did not set out to bring the English constitution in line with 'the rights of man' nor to take a deliberate step towards 'democracy'. It set out to preserve the stability of the state by yielding what it believed to be necessary, to provide, in Norman Gash's words, 'a practical remedy for a felt grievance'.[13] The existing electoral system offended reformers in three principal ways. First, it was impure; and it needed to be purged of its impurity by abolishing the pocket boroughs in which aristocratic patronage was ascendant, by so enlarging the electorate as to make bribery and corruption intolerably expensive and by introducing the secret ballot in order to render voters less obedient to the electoral wishes of their superiors. Second, the system was geographically weighted in favour of the southern part of the country, especially the south-west (nothing damned the old system more than the fact that the 'closed' borough seats at which the will of patrons automatically pre-vailed, about 75 per cent of the total, included only 25 per cent of the borough electorate and that more than half of those small, 'closed' boroughs were in the south-west); balance needed to be restored by shifting some representation to the towns of the north and the midlands. The population of Lancashire, the centre of the cotton-manufacturing industry, whose 'take-off' in the years after 1780 was the most dramatic and most significant aspect of the early industrial revolution, had doubled between 1760 and 1800 and doubled again by 1830. Nor was it simply by population that the imbalance of representation was to be measured. The old system also failed to reflect shifts in the pattern of national wealth-creation. In 1810 England imported 90 million pounds of raw cotton; by 1830 the figure had risen to nearly 250 million. The third defect was that the system was socially exclusive; the electorate needed to be broadened by bringing the middle and lower orders on to the register.

Lord Grey's attention was on the middle classes. He meant, as he later said, to stand by his own order. The primary Whig intention in 1831 was to detach the aggrieved middle classes from the unruly lower classes in order to prevent their joining together in deadly assault on the aristocracy. In 1822 Lord John Russell, one of the committee of four cabinet ministers appointed to draft the reform bill, had enunciated the Whig creed. 'If great changes accomplished by the people are dangerous, although sometimes salutary', he said, when introducing a parliamentary reform motion, 'great changes accomplished by the aristocracy, at the desire of the people, are at once salutary and safe.'[14] The Whigs had been frightened by the stormy popular agitation of the post-Waterloo years on the one hand and by the stern actions taken by the Tory government to suppress it on the other. There were, Lord Holland said in 1819, the year of what came to be called the Peterloo massacre, 'two factions who from very opposite quarters are assailing the free constitution of the country'.[15] Grey and his colleagues came to look upon a substantial measure of parliamentary reform as the necessary price to be paid to prevent moderate, sensible men from leaguing themselves, in despair of any other remedy, with Radical demagogues like William Cobbett and Henry 'Orator' Hunt.[16]

On three notable occasions – the repeal of the Orders-in-Council in 1812, the repeal of the property and income tax in

1816 and the failure of George IV's divorce proceedings against Queen Caroline in 1820 – the Whigs had learned to take party advantage from a swell of public opinion against the government. The success of those three concerted campaigns, the first two accomplished chiefly by mass petitioning, did much to incorporate public opinion into party politics and to make the Whig opposition in the House of Commons the 'instrument of public impatience'.[17] And the very fact (of immense disappointment to the Whigs) that occasional parliamentary victories on the people's behalf did not lead to gains at elections helped to convince the Whigs of the virtues of electoral reform. So did the passing of Catholic emancipation in 1829, which removed from political debate the great issue on which the Whigs had played their traditional role as the protectors of the liberties of the people. Stripped of their 'Catholic' clothing, the Whigs looked to dress themselves in the liberalism of parliamentary reform.

Early in November, before Lord Grey had installed himself in Downing Street, the Whig leader in the House of Commons, Viscount Althorp, told a meeting of the parliamentary party that the opposition was preparing to introduce a reform bill to extend the representation to three large northern towns. So outspoken were the backbenchers, who were in touch with public feeling in their constituencies, in their condemnation of so paltry a measure of reform, that the party leaders were persuaded to abandon it – an instructive example of the power of constituency opinion, normally of little influence, when roused on a great question. Grey returned to his conviction, expressed privately as early as 1820, that 100 borough seats would have to be abolished. He asked the four drafters of the reform bill to bring forth a scheme 'of such a scope and description as to satisfy all reasonable demands, and remove at once, and for ever, all rational grounds for complaint from the minds of the intelligent and independent portion of the community'.[18] That meant, in the language of the day, bringing the middle classes within the pale of the constitution: 'intelligent' and 'independent' were not words used to describe the working class. The Whig bill, intended to drive a wedge between the two classes, became, as it has recently been described, 'a defensive strategy against radical reform'.[19]

It is little wonder, therefore, that the bill, when it was unveiled in the House of Commons on 1 March 1831, startled the House by its seemingly reckless dismantling of the old system. The Whig scheme contained two essential elements. The first was the redistribution of seats. Every borough with a population under 2,000, whether it sent one or two members to Westminster, was to lose its representation. Every borough with a population between 2,000 and 4,000 was henceforth to return only one member. Weymouth's representation was to be reduced from four members to two. In all, those changes would reduce the House of Commons by 168 members. (Boroughmongers who lost their seats received no financial compensation. Pitt, recognising that the sale of seats had created a kind of property in them, had included compensation in his unsuccessful reform bill of 1785. Fifty years on the proposal would have provoked an outcry from the Radicals.) The abolished places were to be partially restored by the creation of new constituencies: two members each were allotted to 22 large English towns – headed by Manchester, Birmingham, Sheffield, Leeds and the London suburbs – and one each to 20 smaller boroughs; 55 new members were given to the English counties (many of them simply being compensated for the abolition of pocket boroughs within their boundaries, but some, like Yorkshire, which was divided into ridings and given six members, being brought into line with their increased population); and nine new seats were found for Wales, Scotland and Ireland.

The second main element was the remodelling of the borough franchise, which was for the first time to be made uniform throughout the country: every £10 householder, that is, every adult male who occupied, either as owner or tenant, premises of an annual value of £10, was to receive the vote. The county franchise was to remain as it was, granted to freeholders whose property carried an annual rental value of 40s. (The act which finally became law in 1832 made three additions to the county franchise, extending the vote to certain copyholders and lease-holders of long residence and, more significant, to any tenant who paid an annual rental of £50 to his landlord. This last, the work of an amendment introduced by the ultra-Tory member for

Buckinghamshire, Viscount Chandos, was the most substantial, direct Tory contribution to the act.)

Those proposals, with the amended county qualifications and some changes in the actual places which lost and gained seats, passed, after a prolonged and tense parliamentary fight, into law.[20] By adding about half a million electors to the rolls, the bill nearly doubled the size of the electorate, which thus came to encompass about 20 per cent of the adult male population. The electorate was thus made roughly to correspond with that portion of the population which could reasonably be identified as the 'political nation'. That may be evidence of the Whigs' sagacity, although it is worth noting that wisdom and self-interest went hand in hand: the newly enfranchised towns, where Dissent and small business were concentrated, formed the Whig Party's electoral backbone for the next four decades; the pocket boroughs which disappeared had long served the Tory interest, in recent elections having returned about three Tories to every opposition member.

Tory opposition to the bill effectively marked the end of that central constituent of Hanoverian politics, 'the party of the crown'. The sweeping abolition of the boroughs frightened all but one or two of the ultra Tories, estranged from the party leadership since 1829, back into the fold; and the whole of the Tory Party mustered against the bill, which passed on its second reading by only 302 votes to 301. The Tories thus found themselves ranged against the crown, since William IV, despite reservations about the bill, gave his full support to ministers. On two occasions he behaved, Grey said, 'like an angel'. The first was in the spring of 1831, when General Gascoigne's amendment opposing any reduction in the total number of seats in England and Wales was carried against the government. Ministers requested a dissolution and the king, rather than dismiss them, granted them the request. The subsequent elections, fought on the slogan, 'the bill, the whole bill, and nothing but the bill', returned a thumping majority for the reformers, even under the old electoral system. That meant that reform was safe in the lower House; the fate of the bill was transferred to the Lords. Throughout the autumn of 1831 and the early

winter of 1832 attempts to reach a compromise between the
government and the large Tory majority in the upper House
came to nothing. William IV then made his second decisive
contribution to events. By promising to consent, if necessary, to
a creation of peers large enough to give the government a
majority in the Lords, he secured the surrender of enough Tory
peers to ensure the bill's passage through the second chamber.

The elections of 1831, the last held under the old system and
the first in English history in which the majority of electors went
to the polls to vote for candidates who pledged themselves to
follow a particular public policy, demonstrated what no one
could have been certain of before the event, that boldness
had earned the Whig government the electorate's enthusiastic
approval. The ultra Tories were smashed and the Tory Party
itself reduced to a borough faction. In the counties and the
popular boroughs Whigs and Radicals swept the field, whereas
of the 204 Tories returned for English constituencies no fewer
than 164 represented boroughs doomed by the reform bill. 'The
Tories could do little', a recent historian has written, 'save
comfort themselves with the wry reflection that never had the
old system shown itself more responsive to public opinion than
when it stood on the brink of extinction.'[21] The bill was not, of
course, well received by all the reformers. Thorough-going
Radicals were disappointed, to varying degrees, by its failure to
introduce shorter parliaments (the maximum life of a parliament
remained seven years), equal electoral districts (a vote in the
more sparsely populated rural seats continued to count for more
than one in a large urban constituency), the removal of property
qualifications for members (the extension of the qualification to
include personal property as well as real property in 1838 was a
small episode in the decline of the landed class' political
hegemony), the payment of members, universal manhood
suffrage and the secret ballot. Those reforms, unmet by the 1832
act, became the famous six points of the Chartists.

The original draft of the bill had included provision for a
secret ballot. The argument in favour of it was that it would
reduce bribery (chiefly a borough practice) at elections. The
argument against it, as Lord Grey put it, was that it was

'inconsistent with the manly spirit and the free avowal of opinion which distinguish the people of England'.[22] That was not the whole of the matter. The 'influence' of the great landowners, which meant, in the counties especially, that whole estates frequently voted as if in a block according to the preference of the landowner, was likely to be more difficult to exercise in a system of secret balloting. The Whigs were not prepared to undermine that 'influence'. Moreover, in an age in which the vote was regarded as a privilege, not a right, men genuinely feared that the civic responsibility which that privilege bestowed on the elector would be lightly observed unless he were visibly accountable for its exercise. Against those considerations the blemish of bribery faded into insignificance. It was, after all, the briber, not the bribed, who required reformation: a secret ballot would enable an elector to accept money from all sides with impunity. What accounted for widespread bribery were the great wealth of the landed class, the high status of a member of parliament and the relatively small size of the electorate. No one disliked the cost of elections – a contested election usually cost about £10,000 for each candidate and occasionally three or four times that amount – more than the candidates and their backers. Had financial considerations been uppermost in men's minds the introduction of the secret ballot would not have been delayed until 1872, by which time the reform act of 1867 had so greatly enlarged the electorate as to make efficient bribery impossible. On financial grounds the retention of open voting ran counter to the whole of the second part of the reform bill, that part being exclusively directed to a variety of measures to reduce the cost of elections.[23] The three chief remedies included in the bill were shortening the duration of polling, increasing the number of polling stations to reduce transport costs and restricting the canvassing area. That section of the bill has received little attention from historians because it provoked little debate in parliament; Whig and Tory landed gentlemen were eager to lessen the financial burden of elections and Radicals were happy to support measures which might go a little way towards preventing the great magnates with large pocketbooks from monopolising the electoral field.

The dropping of the secret ballot by the Whig cabinet had one important consequence. The draft bill had placed the borough franchise at £20, a high qualification specifically intended to ensure 'respectability' among secret balloters. Once the ballot was abandoned, it was deemed safe to lower the qualification to £10. The retention of open voting was therefore, as it turned out, a small price to pay for gaining a greatly expanded electorate.

The Radical bedfellows of the Whigs voted for the bill on the ground that half a loaf from the Whigs was better than no loaf at all from the Tories. The Tory case against the bill received some years ago an ample defence from Professor Gash.[24]

> Almost every point that they made, every fear that they expressed, were good points and well-founded fears, even though the whig majority rejected their validity and denied their justification. Sooner or later all the major prophecies of the opposition came true . . . taken as a whole the tory case against the reform bill was an accurate analysis of the real consequences of reform.

Gash argued that three fundamental Tory objections were vindicated by subsequent events: (1) that the bill would destroy the existing balance of power between king, lords and commons by transferring effective power to the lower House alone; (2) that the bill would divide the country into rural and industrial interests and would therefore shift the political battle away from one conducted between parties towards one conducted between classes; and (3) that by obeying the voice of the people, bowing to the rioters and the Radicals who prophesied revolution if the bill were not carried, the Whigs delivered an awesome weapon into the hands of the people, teaching them that organised opinion, by threatening disorder, could compel government behaviour.

Gash's arguments are open to rejoinders: that the 18th-century balanced constitution was already eroded by the retreat of the crown and the rise of party and that the Lords themselves, by surrendering to the reformers, acknowledged that they had become the junior partner in the legislature; that the division of the country into manufacturing and agricultural interests was a fact of life beyond the remedy of electoral mechanics and that the reform bill, by recognising the claim of the manufacturing towns, helped to reduce potentially explosive tensions between town and country by bringing the conflict between urban tradesmen and the rural gentry more openly into the arena of party politics; and that the Whigs drew up their measures *before* the 1831 riots and that, although they wished to preserve as much aristocratic power as possible, they were not so frightened of the influence of popular opinion on the executive as the Tories were.

The last question, concerning the place of 'the people' in politics, is the heart of the matter. Gash compared the two parties, Whig and Tory, to two physicians, working according to the same science – that is, each upholding the virtue of aristocratic, monarchical government – but differing in their treatment of the particular case. 'If the Whigs had accepted the Tory prognosis, they could scarcely have prescribed the remedy they did.' In a series of articles written after the publication of Gash's book, D. C. Moore argued that the remedy prescribed by the bill was, indeed, a Tory one: that the purpose of the bill, and to a large extent its effect, was to strengthen the landed interest and preserve its political sway. That aristocratic intention was achieved above all, in Moore's view, by two provisions of the bill. One, contained in a clause of the government's own making, sealed off the urban freeholders from the county elec-torate: 40s freeholders in newly enfranchised towns forfeited the right to vote in county elections if they qualified for the borough franchise as £10 householders (the enlargement of some borough boundaries also removed 'suburban' voters from the county registers). The other, a Tory amendment, enfranchised the tenant farmers – Viscount Chandos' £50 tenants-at-will – who were most susceptible to the influence of their superiors, the great landowners.[25] The first device was, indeed, one of the features of the bill; and the second, a direct Tory achievement, had an avowedly aristocratic intention. But that the bill was not, as orthodox opinion has always held it to be, a concession to changing circumstances by a prudent governing class, but rather a tactical offensive designed to hoodwink the nation into leaving the power of that class undiminished, Moore's work has not established.[26] Professor Gash himself, for all his defence of the Tories, accepted the concessionary interpretation. 'What the

Tories said was true', he wrote, 'but what the Whigs did was necessary.' The sentence is disconcerting. For how in politics (or anything else) can things necessary be 'untrue'? Or, to put it another way, how could what the Tories were saying be true (by Gash's argument), since what they chiefly said was that the bill was not necessary?

The great apologist for the Whigs, back in the days when royal absolutism had been made constitutionally impossible, was John Locke. And it was from Locke's two fundamental principles – that government existed to defend property and that effective government rested on the consent of the governed – that the Whigs drew sustenance in the crisis of 1831–32. They were fortunate to have as a spokesman Thomas Macaulay, better known to posterity as a historian than as a member of parliament, whose speech of 2 March 1831 on the reform bill is one of the finest specimens of reasoned oratory in the annals of English politics.[27] The burden of Macaulay's argument was that free institutions cannot continue to function freely unless they have the consent of the governed, assent which will be withdrawn if those institutions fail to accommodate changes in public opinion which are the result of changed circumstances. Macaulay did not challenge the doctrine of government by and for property. The working class had no place in the electorate because, lacking property, it had no permanent stake in the country and would not, therefore, lend a responsible voice to public affairs. (Elsewhere Macaulay once wrote that universal suffrage was 'incompatible with property and . . . consequently incompatible with civilisation'.)[28] What Macaulay pointed out was that the unreformed system was not really government by property at all. It was government by certain fragments of property. And that was a constant danger to the state. 'The great cause of revolutions is this,' he instructed the Tories, 'that while nations move onward, constitutions stand still.' Continue to exclude new forms of property from the constitution and the very purpose of constitutional government, the stability of the state, was imperilled. No system was good if public opinion did not hold it so. Deprived of their natural allies (the owners of land), the owners of other kinds of property would, *faute de mieux*, make common cause with the great enemy of ordered government, the uneducated 'mob'.

Macaulay reminded his audience that only a few months earlier, just across the English Channel, resistance to reform had provoked uprising, the 'July revolution' which had toppled Charles X from the French throne and driven him to take refuge in England. There were revolutionists in England, too, he warned, and the object of the reform bill was to thwart them.

> At present we oppose the schemes of revolutionists with only one half, with only one quarter of our proper force. We say, and we say justly, that it is not by mere numbers, but by property and intelligence, that the nation ought to be governed. Yet, saying this, we exclude from all share in the government great masses of property and intelligence, great numbers of those who are most interested in preserving tranquillity. We do more. We drive over to the side of revolution those whom we shut out from power. Is this a time when the cause of law and order can spare one of its natural allies? . . .
> Now, therefore, while everything at home and abroad forebodes ruin to those who persist in a hopeless struggle against the spirit of the age, now, while the crash of the proudest throne of the Continent is still resounding in our ears . . . Save property divided against itself. Save the multitude, endangered by its own ungovernable passions. Save the aristocracy, endangered by its own unpopular power. . . . The danger is terrible. The time is short. If this bill should be rejected, I pray to God that none of those who concur in rejecting it may ever remember their votes with unavailing remorse, amidst the wreck of laws, the confusion of ranks, the spoliation of property, and the dissolution of social order.

Some modern historians are persuaded that Whig alarmism was not entirely fanciful. Eric Hobsbawm has written that in 1831–32 England, for the first time since the 17th century, found itself in a 'political crisis when something like a revolutionary situation might actually have developed'[29] and E. P. Thompson believes that the country was 'within an ace of revolution'.[30] Certainly both Francis Place, the leader of London radicalism, and Thomas Attwood continually fed cabinet ministers reports of the insurrectionary temper of the populace.[31] And the riots of October 1831 and the 'May Days' of 1832 (when there was undoubtedly extensive armed drilling of the Political Unions and some revolutionary planning) gave substance to their reports.

To describe the reform crisis and its outcome without reference to events outside parliament – especially the remarkable, sustained public enthusiasm for reform kept up by the Political Unions and the press, in London and, more important, in the northern and midland provinces – is inadequate.[32] The Tories' failure to form a government in May 1832 and thus arrest the progress of reform was not simply the result of Peel's refusal to enter a government led by the Duke of Wellington or any other leading Tory. Nor was the House of Lords' surrender in the face of a threatened addition to the peerage simply the graceful conclusion to a courtly dance. The riots of October and the run on the banks' gold reserves in May (almost half of the £3–4 million reserve was withdrawn in the space of two or three days) attested to the determination of sections of the middle classes (many were, of course, horrified by rioting in their towns) to exert irresistible pressure on the government and raised, however remotely, the spectre of social disruption and violence beyond the means of the country's rudimentary police force and local militias to contain. That pressure was, of course, useful to the Whigs, who, like politicians of all ages, were eager to demonstrate the necessity of their case. It also quite genuinely impressed upon them that there was a self-confident power at work in the land whose claim to participation in national politics could no longer be denied.

But that the working class, whose political organisation scarcely existed, was in a position to make common revolutionary cause with the middle classes, or that the leaders of the extra-parliamentary pressure groups would actually have supported a recourse to arms if the bill had failed, may be doubted. In Birmingham, where masters and craftsmen in the metal trades still worked together in small units, Attwood's Political Union was able to bridge the gap between classes; but in the new mill-towns of Lancashire, and in the metropolis, labour and capital were distrustful of each other and found it difficult to cooperate in political action. Francis Place's National Political Union, essentially middle-class in its membership, was from its founding in October 1831 in conflict with the National Union of Working Classes, a body which, inspired by cooperative ideals, utterly repudiated the Whig bill. The nearest that Place came to a revolutionary stance was to call for the run on the banks, and the purpose of that was to demonstrate that there were weapons, in his phrase, 'subtler than arms', but just as powerful.[33] The October riots were uncoordinated, undisciplined manifestations of frustration which did not signal a revolutionary possibility; as Attwood himself allowed, they took place in areas where the influence of the Political Unions was weak. Had the Radical leaders like Place and Attwood been genuine conspirators against the government they would scarcely have taken pains to provide ministers with almost daily 'evidence' of incipient insurrection. They conducted an 'open conspiracy' because their object was to force parliament to pass the reform bill and make revolution unnecessary. They ran, it may be said, the risk of being overtaken by events, of unleashing forces beyond their control. Yet in the end there was no revolution. And since it makes no sense to say that something that did not happen could have happened, history can record only that since there was no revolution, no 'revolutionary situation' existed.

3

THE STRUCTURE OF POST-REFORM POLITICS

In a famous phrase John Bright, the mid-Victorian Radical leader, said of the reform bill that 'it was not a good bill, though it was a great bill when it passed'.[1] What Bright meant was that far more important than the actual terms of the bill were the fact and the manner of its passing. The repeal of the Orders-in-Council and the winning of Catholic emancipation had demonstrated that special interests could achieve their ends by exerting extra-parliamentary pressure on the government and the House of Commons. The reform act demonstrated that the whole of the political nation, backed by the fourth estate and conducting a peaceful campaign that contained a threat within it, could do the same. New rules, so to speak, had come to be applied to the game of politics. Yet the bill itself, even though Lord Grey exaggerated when he called it 'the most aristocratic measure that ever was proposed in Parliament',[2] wrought no immediate revolution in the conduct of electoral or parliamentary politics. The act's chief significance was its acknowledgement of urban, middle-class status; but it did not usher in a period of middle-class political ascendancy over, nor even parity with, the landed elite.

The reform act effected certain mechanical changes in the electoral system, of which three stand out: (1) the size of the electorate was nearly doubled (in Scotland it was raised from just over 4,000 to 65,000, giving that part of the kingdom, as Henry Cockburn, the Edinburgh lawyer who was solicitor-general in Grey's government, remarked, 'a political constitution for the first time')[3] and in most boroughs the new £10 house-holders constituted a majority; (2) there was established for the first time the principle of a uniform qualification for voters in all parts of the country, even though a distinction was made between rural and urban voters; and (3) the imbalance between southern and northern, also between urban and county, representation was partially redressed.

It is true that the boroughs remained over-represented in the new system. The 1833 parliament contained 399 borough members and only 253 county members (the previous figures were 465 and 188), despite the fact that at the 1831 census only 44 per cent of the population was described as living in towns. But as the years went by the increasing urbanisation of England – by mid-century half of the population lived in towns – worked to mitigate that anomaly. Many of the smaller boroughs, moreover, such as market towns or cathedral 'cities', were both economically and socially tied to the surrounding countryside and were essentially agricultural in their habits and outlook. The borough of Huntingdon, for example, with a registered electorate of only 384 persons in 1832 and 390 in 1852, was described in Charles Dod's *Electoral Facts* as having a population 'engaged in the corn, wool and malt trades, in the making of soft cream cheeses . . . and the supply generally of an agricultural district'.[4] There the electoral influence of the Earl of Sandwich remained preponderant. Although 'proprietary boroughs' proper (those that could be bought and sold) disappeared, about 70 members of parliament continued to be returned by boroughs in which a great landowner's influence prevailed.[5] Tories worried that 40s freeholders who lived in the towns, but who continued to vote in county elections, would swamp the rural voters who actually lived in the countryside. Peel, for one, predicted that if the boundary commissioners were to place both Coventry and Birmingham in the northern division of Warwickshire they would effectively give those towns not four, but six, MPs in the House of Commons: 'the landed interest will be overpowered completely'.[6] Events proved him wrong. Both towns were indeed included in North Warwickshire, but that constituency returned two Conservatives at every election between 1832 and the second reform act of 1867.

It is not to belittle the achievement of Grey's government to point out that, great as the long-term moral and political effects of the reform act were, important as the act was in setting Great Britain on the road to electoral democracy, the immediate consequences, whether on the electoral habits of the country or on the social composition of the House of Commons, were far from dramatic.* Bribery and corruption, though they almost certainly diminished after 1832,[7] did not vanish overnight: the House of Commons elected in 1841 earned the soubriquet, 'the bribery parliament'. And although the number of adult males employed in agriculture declined from 32 per cent at the 1831 census to only 21 per cent two decades later, nearly three-quarters of the MPs who sat in the House of Commons in the 1840s were drawn from the aristocracy and gentry, and the remainder included a substantial number of merchants and bankers as well as those proud and wealthy representatives of the new industrial economy, the manufacturers.[8] The old landed and mercantile interests continued to dominate cabinets: of the 103 men who served in cabinets between 1830 and 1866 only 14 could be described as *nouveaux riches*,[9] and of them two, Peel and Gladstone, though their fathers made money from trade, received

---

*The act to abolish slavery in the British empire, passed in the very first session of the reformed parliament, was a rare instance of the direct influence of the reform act on the substance of British politics. The reform act at once increased, at the 1832 elections, the strength of the abolitionist lobby in the House of Commons. The two societies working for abolition – the Agency Committee (formed in 1831) and the older Anti-Slavery Society – managed to extract from 104 successful candidates at the 1832 elections pledges to support immediate abolition. Those members came predominantly from urban boroughs, many of them newly created by the reform act and many of them containing a large Dissenting population – evidence that the reform act, by increasing the size and independence of the electorate, made it easier to bring popular issues to the forefront of an election and compel MPs to have regard to constituency opinion. On the other side, the old West Indian interest, the slave-owners' lobby at Westminster, was drastically diminished in numbers both by the abolition of rotten boroughs and by the defeat of sixteen sitting 'West Indians' at the 1832 elections. In the 1833 parliament the abolitionists outnumbered the 'West Indians' by three to one. (See I. Gross, 'The Abolition of Negro Slavery and British Parliamentary Politics, 1832–3', *Historical Journal*, March, 1980.)

a traditional upper-class education. Each of them went up from public school to Christ Church, Oxford, the most Tory and aristocratic of Oxbridge colleges, and each carried off a double first. Melbourne's cabinets of 1834 and 1835 were the only ones between 1832 and 1852 to contain more commoners than peers, though it is true that throughout the period the more important offices were usually filled by the former. 'We are a servile, aristocracy-loving, lord-ridden people', Richard Cobden, the Radical member of parliament and opponent of primogeniture and entail, lamented in 1849.[10]

One of the most important reasons why the landed class retained its parliamentary sway was the undiminished cost of becoming a member of parliament. As late as 1864 the *Economist* estimated that the possibility of pursuing a career in politics was limited to a very small class numbering about 5,000, and it had no doubt that the cost entailed in getting elected and in living in the manner required of an MP was the principal obstacle in the way of would-be middle-class politicians.[11] Politics was a money-spending, not a money-making, occupation. Partly for the same reason the number of uncontested elections remained high. Between 1832 and 1852 there were 501 elections in the 67 English and Welsh county constituencies and 62 per cent of them were uncontested; in some counties, like the Tory-held ones of Caernarvonshire, Montgomeryshire and Pembrokeshire, there was not a single contest during the whole period. Even so, the average number of contested elections at the five general elections held after 1832 was twice that at the five elections held between 1807 and 1830. Not every uncontested election, moreover, was evidence of political torpor. In two-member constituencies the absence of a contest often signified that a Whig/Tory division of the spoils was so certain an outcome that a contest would merely involve the two sides in needless expense. Often, too, a real contest took place during the canvass of electors before polling day, only for one side, accepting defeat, to retire before the actual poll, again, to avoid the expense of treating electors and transporting them to the polling stations. In those circumstances what had been a hard fight would appear in the records as an 'uncontested' election.

The tendency of voters to follow the wishes of their landlords remained. In many places election returns mirrored so faithfully the pattern of land ownership that it would be possible to draw a topography of the estates from the evidence of the pollbooks alone. At the South Lincolnshire election of 1841, for example, in 32 of the 44 parishes owned by a single landowner every vote was cast on the landowner's side.[12] Whig and Tory alike, in constituencies in which the ownership of land was more or less equally balanced between them, were happy to maintain the 'peace of the county' by agreeing to share the representation. This return to normalcy was a factor in the Conservative revival after the heightened partisanship displayed at the 1831 and 1832 elections, and that the Whigs were as happy to return to it as their rivals may be illustrated by the course of events at Northamptonshire. Before the election of 1831 the county's two seats had been shared between the parties; in 1831 two reformers were returned; the new act divided the county into northern and southern divisions and increased its representation to four members. At the first elections under the new dispensation some ardent reformers in the locality were eager to win all four seats. To do so would entail contests in both divisions of the county, and Viscount Althorp, the Whig leader in the House of Commons and member for the county, reacted angrily to the suggestion, unwilling as he was to 'go to some absurd expense, because some wrongheaded people choose it and insist upon dragging me into it against all reason and common sense'.[13] Radical reformers looked upon the reform act as the starting-point for a thorough remodelling of the country's social and economic institutions; conservative-minded Whigs like Althorp were apt to look on it more as the conclusion of a long battle against the old system. Althorp's affable readiness to restore the Tories to their county inheritance is a telling illustration, all the more for his being a party leader, of the truth that Whigs and Tories were more joined by common membership of the landed class than divided by party rivalry. Small wonder is it that William Hazlitt once described the two parties as coaches rumbling along the same road to the same destination, splashing each other with mud as they went.[14]

The 'influence' wielded by the great landowners and the response which it evoked – the much-vaunted 'deference' of the electorate, though that deference owed as much to the entirely natural product of generations of English life, the predeliction, namely, among rural people to respect a squire and broad acres more than a merchant banker and a lavish new country house – robbed many mid-19th-century county elections of genuine political content. 'For the typical tenant on a rural estate', an historian has recently written, 'the vote was an intermittent function of his membership of the community and not a matter of personal responsibility . . . the tenant's primary responsibility was towards his landlord, not his conscience; and his primary loyalty was to the estate, not a political party.'[15] Yet it is undoubtedly so that for the most part what historians have called 'deference' was, simultaneously, a sharing of attitudes, a coincidence of opinions between landlord and tenant. About the great issues of high politics, such as the maintenance of the privileges of the Church of England and the defence of the landed interest, landlords and tenants (in England at least) had no quarrel. That is one of the fundamental reasons why the great landowners, Whig and Tory, were able to exercise continued influence over the electorate. It does not follow that, because tenants did not often take issue with the politics of their landlords, they had no political opinions at all. Neither the severe Tory losses at the elections of 1831 and 1832 nor, later, the farmers' revolt against free trade in corn would have been possible had not the rural electorate, somnolent perhaps in ordinary times, become roused when it felt the need. That being so, what reason, other than the pomposity of the so-called 'politically informed', can be brought to sustain the argument that in following their landlords' preferences in quiet times, rural voters behaved apolitically? On what ground can their acquiescence, since it was not automatic, be scorned when it suited their purposes?

County electioneering remained, after 1832, much as it had been; in the boroughs the tempo of party politics picked up. The difference is partly explained by the effect of the registration clauses in the reform act. For the first time in English history every eligible voter was required to have his name placed on an electoral register. Since the matter of sorting out who was eligible as a £10 householder or who as a 40s freeholder, or in the counties who as a leaseholder or copyholder or £50 tenant-at-will, there was much work for the attorneys to do. And since a name once on the list remained there, rightfully or not, unless it were challenged, there was incentive for the parties to flood the lists with names of their own supporters and file claims against persons registered by their opponents. By the mid-1830s both parties had registration associations all over the country. 'We must organise our associations in London to work the Reform Bills', Joseph Parkes, a Whig election manager, wrote in 1835, 'to point out to the country the facility and effect of organization, pre-arrangement and funds by small annual subscriptions for registration especially.'[16] Activity was much greater in the boroughs than the counties, because there registration was annual, arousing political excitement every twelve months (county electors had to register only once), and because there, too, the municipal reform act of 1835, which abolished the predominantly Tory, self-electing, oligarchic town corporations and introduced a democratic, rate-paying franchise, had a similar effect.

In the counties new forms of political organisation, independent of the existing social and economic ties, were hardly necessary. Sufficient organisation to carry political communications and to get voters to the polls were already provided by the hierarchy of estate management: the estate agent, or manager, simply added the political duty to his other obligations. Borough society, ranging from paupers to great merchant princes, was amorphous, bound together by few of the ties which unified agrarian society. Urban distinctions of rank were more finely graded than rural ones, the variety of occupations and incomes far greater, so that to unite the diverse groups composing the borough electorate in a common political purpose required an independent, superimposed, explicit political organisation. Dr Nossiter's analysis of nineteen towns has shown the post-1832 urban electorate to have been engaged largely in 'pre-industrial revolution' employment: shopkeepers, skilled artisans, professional people and merchants. 'In electorates of this nature', he has concluded, 'there cannot have been many seriously exposed to external pressure to vote against their inclinations; and as so many were in occupations requiring clerical ability the vast majority must have been sufficiently educated to have political views of their own.'[17] Moreover, although it is true that the party struggle was not so much between capital and labour as, in a very general way, it was between the urban manufacturer/artisan set and the old merchant/landed gentleman elite, an antagonism intensified by the corresponding battle between Nonconformity and the Church,[18] and although it is also true that the party struggle was carried on in the boroughs chiefly by middle-class activists, nevertheless the rapid expansion of the population (the doubling of the nation's population between 1800 and 1850 equalled *all* previous growth) brought the most salient and difficult social problems of the age – poverty, illiteracy, drunkenness, child labour, pollution, unemployment – most acutely, or at any rate most overtly, to bear in the crowded towns.

The effect of all this went far beyond the occasional spectacle of a parliamentary election (though the heightened party feelings of the 1830s were sustained by the remarkable occurrence of six general elections between 1830 and 1841, more than in any other decade in British history). The struggle to gain control of the vestry (the most important institution of local government), of the board of guardians responsible for administering the poor law and of the local council was unceasing. That continual fight carried politics into everyday life, just as the quarrels which broke out over parochial matters were carried over into national politics. The 'politicising of minor institutions', as one historian has recently described it, is one of the defining features of early Victorian politics.[19] The process began, indeed, before 1830, largely because *parvenu* manufacturers and the like, often Dissenters, were barred from positions of social and political leadership commensurate with their economic status (because their towns were unrepresented in parliament and the Anglican/Tory town corporations were closed to them), and therefore they chose the parish vestry – the ancient assembly of ratepayers which had powers of taxation to provide for a number of parish responsibilities, chiefly the upkeep of Church buildings and the relief of the poor – as the object of their political ambition. 'Hence in many places a Liberal or radical vestry emerged as a political counterweight to a Tory oligarchy as part of a battle between rival élites within the urban middle class.'[20] The vestry's power to levy a Church rate, paid by all ratepayers whatever their faith for the maintenance of Anglican churches, was a potent source of parochial political antagonism and a fundamental ingredient in the electoral alliance, both locally and nationally, between Whig/Liberalism and Dissent. The administration of the poor law was equally contentious. 'Political party feeling prevails to a mischievous extent at Leeds', an assistant poor law commissioner reported in 1841; 'the parties are nearly balanced and it is scarcely possible to take any step in Leeds township without exciting strong party feeling.'[21]

In the 1830s and 1840s the great issues of national politics – the privileges of the Church of England, the new poor law of 1834, the tariff on imported agricultural goods and the host of problems arising from industrial growth and urban squalor – were at the centre of local rivalries between Dissenter and Churchman, millowner and squire. Divisions on those questions were as sharp at elections to local boards as they were in the debating chambers at Westminster. It is not surprising, therefore, that local election results tended to correspond closely to the rise and fall of party fortunes in parliament. The changing party balance in the town councils at Liverpool and Leeds, for example, mirrors the rise and fall of the Conservative Party from the beginning of its recovery in 1835 to its break-up over the repeal of the corn laws in 1846. The steady electoral advance of the party in the 1830s, culminating in the overwhelming victory gained at the elections of 1841, which gave Peel's party a majority of nearly 100 in the House of Commons, was matched by Conservative progress at local elections.

The initiative to form local party organisations came, not from the centre, but from the constituencies themselves. The registration societies, both Liberal and Conservative (the party names which came to predominate in the 1830s, though 'Whig' survived to indicate an aristocratic tradition distinct from Liberal-

Local Election Results[22]

	Liverpool		Leeds	
	Liberal	Conservative	Liberal	Conservative
1835	43	5	39	9
1837	34	14	33	15
1841	15	33	23	25
1847	14	34	33	15
1852	18	30	40	8

ism and Radicalism and 'Tory', as a term of both affection and abuse, has never fallen into disuse), which proliferated after 1832 were the fruit of local endeavour. In the counties, where as late as 1874 Conservative Associations existed in barely more than half the constituencies, the local autonomy of the leading families was not to be overborne by party managers at Westminster. And even in the boroughs the financing of registration, the selection of candidates and the organisation of the canvass was, except in exceptional circumstances, left to local zealots. The heads of the parties were reluctant to soil their hands in humdrum electoral business, especially if, like Lord Stanley, a reformer in 1832 but by 1841 one of Peel's right-hand men, they worried about the damage which would be done to the conduct of national life by the effort to 'organise the whole country in such a manner that every man must be a partisan'. The damage that Stanley feared – his fear goes part of the way towards explaining the Whigs' irresolution as the 1830s went by and the parallel revival of Conservative self-confidence – was the kindling of the spark of democracy into a conflagration.[23] More common was the response of the Tory, Charles Wynne, who disliked political associations, but who helped to establish a Conservative Society in Denbighshire because 'in the circumstances of the present time' there was 'utility in acquiescing in what one cannot prevent'.[24]

Present circumstances were, in the aftermath of the reform crisis, more pressing for the Conservatives than the Whigs, reduced as they were at the 1832 elections to a rump of about 150 MPs in the House of Commons. The crown no longer had the means or the authority to deliver a parliamentary majority to the government of its choice. In 1834 William IV dismissed the Whigs, who commanded a majority in the Commons, only to discover a few months later that he had no choice but to take them back. In 1841 the Whig government of Lord Melbourne, granted a dissolution by Queen Victoria, was defeated at the polls – the first time, as Melbourne himself put it, that the crown had a majority returned 'smack against it'. It was no accident that the first permanent central party organisation, the Carlton Club, was established by the Conservatives in 1832. Soon enough, however, reverses at the 1835 elections demonstrated to the Whigs that they, too, needed to put their house in order. The Reform Club, which became the centre of activity for Whigs, Liberals and Radicals – for anyone opposed to the Conservatives – was founded in 1836. Those two central bodies, the Carlton and the Reform, served as social clubs as well as management offices for the two parties and their political functions were limited. They raised small amounts of money to disburse to especially needy parliamentary candidates; they collected information about the state of the registers; very occasionally they offered to supply a candidate to a constituency in distress. But their significance lay less in what they actually accomplished and more in the future direction of party organisation to which they pointed and the excited state of party warfare in the 1830s to which they bore tribute.

The institutionalising of party was also taking place in Ireland, where by the time of the 1832 elections the Protestant Conservative Association already provided the Conservatives with an industrious central headquarters. It held weekly meetings, directed press operations and raised a weekly subscription of nearly £600. Irish Whiggery, or Liberalism, was less homogenous, because it needed to accommodate the Radical supporters of Daniel O'Connell and his Repeal Association. Repeal of the union was as distasteful to English Whigs as it was to Tories. But even though O'Connell fought the 1832 elections on the repeal issue, the repealers remained a strand within Liberalism, not a separate party. Repeal candidates did not stand against Whig candidates; it was simply that where the nationalist sentiment was strong, they stood, in place of more orthodox Whig candidates, on the government interest and against the Tories. 'Serious though the divergences of opinion within the liberal party might be', J. H. Whyte has written, 'none of them was as important as the line of cleavage which separated all liberals from the conservatives. The two-party system was in Irish constituencies the rule: that was the system to which the Irish people were becoming accustomed.'[25]

Ideas and party achieved an intelligible and recognisable identification in the 1830s. The internal divisions between liberal Conservatism and ultra Toryism, on the one hand, and between conservative Whiggery and advanced Liberalism, on the other, did not disappear. But they were more or less absorbed in the rivalry between the two great parties themselves, a rivalry which expressed itself most intensely in the debate about the future of the established Church. The litmus test of whether a man were a Whig or a Conservative was his attitude to the Church. In May 1834 four Whig cabinet ministers, led by Lord Stanley and Sir James Graham, separated themselves from the party by resigning from Grey's government rather than assent to the principle that parliament had the authority to appropriate surplus revenues of the Irish Church (the established, Anglican Church in Ireland) to secular purposes. But Stanley's attempt to form a centre party of his own, the 'Derby dilly' as O'Connell contemptuously called it, was dashed on the rock of the two-party system. By 1837 all of his followers (40-strong at their peak) had either returned to the Whig fold or made their way across the floor of the Commons (as he and Graham did) into the ranks of the Conservatives. In 1834, too, William IV, after dismissing the Whig government in November, sought to replace it by a coalition of right-wing Whigs and moderate Conservatives. His object was the same as Stanley's: to banish the Radicals and ultra Tories to the sidelines and leave the field to men of the centre; more specifically, to block the projected assault on Irish Church revenues, which he deemed 'a step to the subversion of the English as well as the Irish establishment and also an attack on the principle of property'.[26] Peel and Melbourne, the leaders of the two parties, each told the king that his scheme was fanciful.

Peel explained to him that, after divisions within the cabinet on *issues* had broken up the Whig government, it was impossible to imagine that a government drawing its members from opposing parties could endure.[27]

The year from the spring of 1834, when Grey's government entered the throes of its dissolution, to the spring of 1835, when Peel was forced to abandon the attempt to carry on a minority Conservative administration, was one of exceptionally high political tension. It is not surprising that a distinguished Prussian visitor to England should have written home in April 1835, apologising for having spoken so much of politics in his letters, but defending himself by pointing out that in England the very atmosphere was 'impregnated with politics': 'you are obliged to draw them in with the air you breathe'.[28] On the night that Peel's government left office, the same visitor, Professor Raumer, a distinguished historian and public servant, was at a grand dinner in London and he used the occasion to instruct his continental friends in the temper of English politics.

> In this very same hour the ministry was dissolved; and this dissolution was not (as it so often is in France) a mere concern of *cotéries* and *tracasséries*, but had a real substantive meaning, and tended to real and efficient changes. What a deal of wit, good and bad – what angry passions – what hope and fear – what praise and blame – would have foamed over, like *champagne mousseux*, in such an hour, in Paris! Here, not a trace of the kind. . . . It seemed as if all that was passing without were but a light ripple on the surface of the waters. The weal of England, her riches, her laws, her freedom, seemed moored to some immovable anchor in the securest and serenest depths of the ocean, whence neither winds nor waves can ever tear them loose. The clouds which flit along the face of heaven, and so often seem, to us timid spectators, to portend a coming storm, may here be regarded as but the passing fleeces of a summer sky.[29]

For a generation and more Englishmen had been accustomed to hear that revolution was at their doorstep; and the ruling classes were just then about to have their steel tested by the clamorous agitation of factory reformers, anti-poor law protesters and Chartists. Yet to a foreign observer, marvelling at the wealth of England and envying her constitutional liberty, what was striking was the security of the ruling classes and their unshaken belief in their own permanence, freeing them to quarrel amicably among themselves and play the game of politics in a gentlemanly manner.

Organisational advances and a hardening of party loyalties were changing the rules of the game. In the House of Commons real independence was already becoming a luxury of the past by 1830. In the following decade it almost completely disappeared.[30] It is true that the notion of 'party membership' had not yet lodged itself in the English political mind, so that the party whips on both sides of the House of Commons had great difficulty in deciding to which MPs should be sent circular letters asking for their attendance and votes, not wishing to offend some by presuming on their support, others by seeming to disdain it. But in 1839 Francis Bonham, the Conservative election manager, was able to identify only five 'doubtfuls' (MPs who were not clearly aligned with one side of the House or the other) and even them he described as '*now* rather Conservative'.[31]

The story was the same in the House of Lords, where the 'party of the crown' (members who supported the king's ministers whatever their political complexion, simply because they *were* the king's ministers) was, for the first time, almost invisible. 'All are either Whigs or Tories', the diarist, Charles Greville, who was clerk to the privy council, wrote, 'arrayed against each other and battling for power.'[32] The change was actually less dramatic than it appeared, because during the 50 years of Tory rule from Pitt to Wellington many peers, notably the bishops, had been able to hide their Tory sympathies behind the 'party of the crown' mask. When the Whigs became the party of government the mask was ripped off and their Toryism uncovered. Only two bishops among the 30 spiritual peers, for instance, voted with the Whig government when the Lords threw out the reform bill in 1831.

The sharpened outlines of party in the House of Lords coincided with the decline of the upper chamber's authority in the state. Abolishing the nomination boroughs meant taking from the peers their hand-picked representatives in the Commons and widening the franchise gave the lower House a title to representative legitimacy which raised its status far above that of the House of Lords. The Conservative majority in the Lords was able, in the late 1830s, to thwart or adulterate a number of measures successfully carried through the Commons by the Whig government. That was not quite the last show of effective power which the Lords exercised in British history. (As late as 1893 the Lords, exercising what Lord Salisbury called their 'referendal' function of blocking measures which they believed to want the approval of the majority of the electorate, threw out Gladstone's Irish Home Rule bill.) But it became a catchphrase of the age that 'a collision between the two Houses' could not be endured with safety to the state; and, by and large, it was the Lords who were expected to steer clear of it. In 1846, when the Lords, august assembly of great landowners, consented with remarkable equanimity to the repeal of the corn laws, they did so, in part at least, because they had no answer to the purely constitutional argument which the Duke of Wellington (doing his best, it is true, by the government of which he was an adornment) put plainly to them.

> We know that, if we should reject this Bill, it is a Bill which has been agreed to by the other two branches of the Legislature; and that the House of Lords stands alone in rejecting this measure. Now that, my Lords . . . is a position in which you cannot stand, because you are entirely powerless; without the House of Commons and the Crown, the House of Lords can do nothing.[33]

The stiffening of party loyalties at Westminster had its parallel in the country. Electors scrutinised MPs' votes in the House of Commons more closely than before and one Conservative declared, in 1836, that whereas ten years earlier most of the educated classes had been politically neutral, the 'whole nation' was now split into two great opposing parties.[34] In two-member constituencies the practice of split-voting at elections (that is, an elector's casting his two votes for candidates of rival parties) fell into virtual abeyance, as the figures for three middle-sized constituencies illustrate.

Whether the Conservatives were better organised than their opponents and whether, if they were, that superiority played a decisive part in their performance at the 1837 and 1841 elections are questions difficult to answer. There is some reason to believe

Percentage of Split-Voting at Three Boroughs[35]

	1830 elections	1837 elections	1841 elections
Lewes	52.9	5.0	2.9
Maidstone	33.2	9.6	1.0
Northampton	43.0	7.6	9.8

that they had more money, but little to suggest that they were more efficient at getting their supporters on to the registers. But whatever the explanation for it, the Conservative triumph in 1841 was a landmark in British political development. 'The Conservatives between 1832 and 1841', Professor Gash has written, 'were the first example in British parliamentary history of a party which organized itself for electoral victory and forced its leaders into office against the wishes of the Crown by winning a majority in a general election.'[36] It is a striking sentence which accurately and tersely sums up the developments which make the decade after the reform act the formative years of the modern British parliamentary system: a fight for supremacy in the House of Commons between organised parties, acting independently of royal favour or royal wishes and recognising that the source of that supremacy was an electorate whose sentiments, however difficult they might be to decipher, were becoming of cardinal importance in politics. The battle of ideas in the 1830s, which drove the cabinet which had been gathered around Lord Grey in 1830 apart and which united the Conservatives in resistance to the forward aims of liberalism, sustained the organisational advances of the decade and ended in the rehabilitation of Conservatism.

4

THE WHIG DECADE

The decade of party strife which began with a huge Whig majority in 1832 and ended in Conservative triumph in 1841 was marked by the development of a constitutional principle which was not entirely new, but which had never before operated with such force: the notion that a government was responsible to parliament for the legislative measures which it laid before it. The word 'programme' still lay in the future, but the Whigs' difficulties in the 1830s stemmed in great part from, or manifested themselves as, the failure to devise and carry through parliament a range of public policies able to command the assent of parliament and meet the aspirations of a majority of the electorate. In the past a government had fallen (when it was not the victim of royal whim) from mismanagement, from a realignment of parliamentary 'connexions' or groups of 'friends', or from the destabilising effects of a crisis. It did not fall from the failure to satisfy a variety of interests and its fall was not preceded by a war of attrition in which its strength slowly dwindled at successive elections.

The Whig governments of the 1830s did nothing especially wrong: they did not notably, nor corruptly, mismanage the nation's business (although Lord Grey was forced to give way to Lord Melbourne after a mishandling of the government's private negotiations with the Irish leader, Daniel O'Connell, in 1834); nor did any crisis – foreign, financial or constitutional – suddenly break upon them and destroy them. Their majority was simply whittled away: from 150 MPs after the 1832 elections the Conservative numbers rose to about 290 in 1835, then 313 in 1837 (so that for the last four years of Whig government the parties were very nearly balanced) and, finally, 370 in 1841. The Whig position was never so powerful as the returns at the 1832 elections suggested, since the 'supporters of government' were by no means all Whigs, but included more than 100 Radicals of varying hues, chief among them O'Connell's 'Brigade' of Irish nationalists and a knot of Benthamites or 'Philosophic Radicals'. Among the government's supporters were also a number of conservative-minded Whigs, men who accepted the necessity of parliamentary reform in 1831–32, but who were nervous of any further progress towards the implementation of a radical 'programme'. Between those two poles the Whigs had a difficult course to chart and their gradual decline – of the kind which has ever since threatened to afflict governments in a democratic party system – was the consequence of their inability to please everyone all of the time. The 1830s are the first period in English history to whose electoral behaviour the metaphor of the 'swing of the pendulum' may be usefully applied. More than anything else the parallel movement of the Whigs downwards and the Conservatives upwards marks the birth of modern, two-party politics.

On the eve of their demise, in May 1841, the Whigs placed before parliament a bill to alter the tariff duties on the import of sugar into Great Britain. It was an important financial and imperial measure, affecting as it did the revenue of the country and relations between Great Britain and the sugar colonies in the Caribbean. The bill was defeated in the House of Commons by 36 votes; and the Conservative opposition, seeing that the government meant neither to resign nor to ask for a dissolution of parliament and put itself to the test of electoral judgement, introduced a motion of no-confidence in the government in the House of Commons. Ministers, Robert Peel told the House, did 'not sufficiently possess the confidence of the House of Commons to enable them to carry through the House measures which they deem of essential importance to the public welfare' and 'their continuance in office, under the circumstances, is at variance with the spirit of the constitution'.[1] In reply Macaulay met Peel's argument face on. The House lost confidence in a government, he asserted, when it believed ministers to be no longer able to administer the existing law: it could not be interpreted as loss of confidence 'if the House withheld its assent from any new legislative measure, or refused to sanction the alteration of an old law'.[2] Macaulay had historical precedent on his side, but it was Peel who, by the very novelty of stating his doctrine so baldly, judged contemporary attitudes the more finely. Governments were, by 1841, expected to innovate; they were looked to to provide adjustments in the law to accommodate changes in social and economic relationships. In a celebrated phrase near the end of the century Sir William Harcourt is reputed to have said, 'we are all socialists now'. The statement (if it was made) was nonsense; but it expressed a truth. In the same spirit a Conservative might have said in the 1830s, 'we are all reformers now'. The 1830s have long been known as the 'decade of reform'; and even if the achievements of the decade no longer seem to historians entirely to eclipse those of the 1820s, the title is apt, for it was then that the expectation that every government, whatever its party label, would be a reforming one took root.

Peel's 'Tamworth Manifesto' of 1834 acknowledged the fact.[3] When Melbourne's government was abruptly dismissed by William IV at the end of 1834, Peel hurried back from a vacation in Italy to take up the reins of government. He was granted a dissolution by the king and his so-called manifesto (the word appears nowhere in the document) was really nothing more, in its form, than an open letter to his Tamworth constituents such as every candidate in those days issued at the beginning of his canvass. Its language and its implications, however, were broader than usual, because Peel took the opportunity to enunciate the general principles on which he intended to conduct the Conservative government which he had just been called upon to form. The manifesto, which was approved by the new cabinet before it was released to the national press, sought to distance Conservatism (the party had deliberately adopted the new term) from the old-fashioned and somewhat static Toryism associated in the public mind with the Duke of Wellington, who had briefly served as a kind of 'caretaker' prime minister while Peel was making his way back to England. It made what Peel called a 'frank and explicit' appeal to 'that class which is much less interested in the contentions of party, than in the maintenance of order and the cause of good government'; and it also announced that a Conservative government would have no desire to disturb the reform settlement of 1832 and would, in the spirit of the reform act, conduct a careful review of institutions, civil and ecclesiastical, in a friendly temper, in order to correct 'proved abuses' and redress 'real grievances'. The language may seem mild a century-and-a-half later, but it was artfully chosen both to warn the ultra Tories in Peel's own party that they should not expect him to lead them in a course of reaction and to tempt those moderates who had stood by Lord Grey during the reform battle, but who had since been disquieted by the radical tendencies of the Whig government, especially on matters relating to Ireland and the established Church.

Grey's government, though its historic task was completed with the passing of the reform act, did not rest on its laurels. The abolition of slavery throughout the empire in 1833 redeemed the pledges given by many Whig candidates at the elections of 1830; the grant of £20,000 in the same year to the several voluntary societies which provided elementary education established the principle, though the amount of money was puny, of state-assisted education; the 1833 factory act (which applied only to the textile industry), by limiting the number of hours that young persons could work in the mills and by establishing an inspectorate with the duty of seeing that the act was enforced,[4] laid the foundation of subsequent industrial and social legislation; and the lord chancellor, Henry Brougham, presided over a reform of the law more extensive than any since the 17th century and added lustre to an already renowned career by establishing the central criminal court and the Judicial Committee of the Privy Council.[5] The reforms of 1833 were followed by the new poor law of 1834, one of the great controversial measures in 19th-century social history, but in the reduction which it was expected to bring to the amount paid in poor rates by the owners of property so to the liking of a still overwhelmingly landed parliament that it attracted only a handful of opponents there.

The measure for the abolition of slavery disappointed humanitarians by delaying full emancipation to the slaves until a period of 'apprenticeship' in limited freedom had been served (seven years for slaves who worked on the land, five years for the rest) and by giving £20,000,000 to the slave-owners in compensation for the loss of their 'property'. Nor did the factory act, which restricted itself to child labour, go nearly far enough to satisfy them. And the new poor law, with its provision for placing in a workhouse able-bodied paupers who did not find employment, raised a storm of protest which merged with the campaigns for universal manhood suffrage and a ten-hour day in the textile mills in the great Chartist agitation of the late 1830s and early 1840s.

The Whigs were not in a position, even had they been of a mind, to satisfy the ambitions of the Radicals. Between 1832 and 1837 at least 40 MPs who had voted for the reform act made their way across the floor of the House of Commons to the opposition benches. The danger to the party's tenure of office came from the right, not the left. Inside parliament, the English Radicals, who had no leader and were deeply divided among themselves, never formed a coherent group and by 1837 they were difficult to distinguish, so far as their influence on proceedings in the House of Commons went, from the more forward spirits within Whiggery itself. Outside parliament, those people who pressed for a further extension of the franchise to include the working man or for the repeal of the new poor law and the statutory enforcement of a ten-hour day in the factories had, being themselves without the franchise, little electoral infuence. Indeed, during the six years of Lord Melbourne's government, which lasted from 1835 to 1841, the most damaging charge levelled against the Whigs (whatever its truth) was not that they had forsaken radicalism, but that they were wagged by their Radical tail. It both alarmed the Conservative opposition and gave it the scent of electoral victory that the tail, or at any rate the most visible part of it, was Irish and Roman Catholic.

The Irish question, directly and indirectly, brought down

more governments in the 19th century than any other cause. By the time that the Whigs came into office in 1830 it had already driven Pitt from office in 1801 and the 'Talents' in 1806; and the granting of Catholic emancipation in 1829 by the Duke of Wellington's government had so gravely weakened Tory unity as to be the proximate cause of his departure a year later. The essence of the Irish grievance was this, that a land-starved peasantry and tenantry (Ireland's population grew more rapidly than that of any other European nation in the first half of the 19th century) paid rents to landlords who were preponderantly English, Protestant and absent, and that a population overwhelmingly Roman Catholic (about 80 per cent of the people) was compelled by law to support, by tithes and taxes, a wealthy, overmanned, alien clerical establishment, the Church of Ireland. That Church had only 850,000 members, less than the one English diocese of Durham, yet it had eighteen bishops and four archbishops. It drew from the Irish peasantry an annual revenue of £800,000, three-quarters of which came from the hated tithe.

> The Irish difficulty [G. M. Young wrote] went deeper than the philosophy of the age could reach. The twin cell of English life, the squire administering what everybody recognizes as law and the parson preaching what everybody acknowledges to be religion, had no meaning in a country where the squire was usually an invader and the parson always a heretic. England had staked the good government of Ireland on a double speculation, that the Irish would conform to the Protestant establishment and that they would accept the English use of landlord, farmer and labourer. The Irishry preferred to misgovern themselves as Catholics and small-holders.[6]

In the same month that Lord Grey took office a 'tithe war' began in Ireland. Throughout 1831 the 'war', which was the refusal of tenants and sub-tenants to pay the tithe, gathered momentum; and by 1832 it had taken on the aspect of a general, and violent, assault on landlordism and property. According to the official figures crimes in Ireland in 1832 included 568 acts of incendiarism (against crops and farm buildings) and 290 cattle-maimings.[7] Troops sent by the government to compel payment of the tithe were powerless to extract arrears from farmers who had not the means to pay them. Against that background the organisation by Daniel O'Connell – the 'uncrowned king' of Ireland – of a nationalist movement to repeal the act of union (1801) between Great Britain and Ireland and restore a parliament to Dublin took on a sombre colouring in the eyes of English unionists. O'Connell preached non-violent, constitutional agitation and his followers practised what he preached. The 'Irish Volunteers' were not to be found among the bands who roamed the countryside committing outrages. But the double face of Irish discontent – an uncontrolled wave of agrarian lawlessness and a well-organised, brilliantly-led political movement with a band of 35 or 40 MPs at Westminster who had pledged themselves at the 1832 elections to the repeal of the union – presented an alarming prospect to the imperial government.

In 1833, therefore, Edward Stanley, the Irish secretary, introduced into parliament a bill to make public meetings for a political purpose illegal without the permission of the lord-lieutenant of the county, to authorise the search of private dwellings without warrant, to substitute courts-martial for civil courts and to suspend habeas corpus. That was coercion. The other half of the government's policy, the conciliation, was a bill to reform the Irish Church. Coercion angered the Irish, but at least it placated the Conservative opposition. Conciliation satisfied neither the Irish nationalists nor the Conservatives. The bill that passed into law in 1833 made some useful reforms. Two of the four archbishoprics and ten of the bishoprics were abolished, reducing the number of Anglican sees from 22 to 10. Any benefice so destitute of worshippers that no service had been held for three years was also abolished. And the cess, a tax levied on parishioners for the upkeep of church buildings (the equivalent of the Church rate in England) was replaced by a graduated income tax on the clergy. The saving from those measures was £150,000 annually, the so-called 'surplus revenue' of the Irish Church.

The question was, what was to be done with the money, especially the money expected from the sale of leases on defunct episcopal lands. The Whig bill proposed, in the famous clause 147, that an ecclesiastical commission be appointed to supervise the funds. It left open the question whether they should be spent on religious or secular objects. Irish Radicals, English Dissenters and the more progressive wing of the government were, by and large, in favour of their use for secular purposes, what went by the name of 'lay appropriation'. In their eyes the very point of the reform was to reduce the wealth of the Church, hated symbol of English tyranny, in order to release money for schemes to improve the condition, especially the education, of Irish Roman Catholics. As it stood, clause 147 permitted, though it did not prescribe, the lay appropriation of surplus funds. That was sufficient to alarm the Conservatives, who saw in lay appropriation an attack on private property, an advance towards the disestablishment of the Irish Church (and, indirectly, of the Church in England, whose disestablishment was a leading object of the Dissenters), a surrender to popery and a step in the direction of the repeal of the union. 'Everything Protestant in Ireland is English', the *Times* thundered three years later, when the controversy was still raging; 'it rests on Great Britain, and clings to her, and constitutes the only bond of union between these islands. Everything Popish is anti-English – it rests on animosity towards Great Britain, clings to the hope of separation from her, and constitutes the only vulnerable spot in the British Empire, the sole element of weakness and of ruin.'[8]

Property and the Protestant religion found their defenders in the Tory peers, who threw out clause 147 when the bill reached the House of Lords. The government wanted the resolve to restore it and so the Irish Church bill passed into law, not as a great national measure for Ireland, but as a tinkering with the administration of the Anglican establishment. O'Connell repudiated it on behalf, as he said, of the people of Ireland. 'The pith, substance, the marrow and essence of the bill is plucked out of it, and the husk, the rind, the void and valueless shell, the shrivelled and empty skin, is left behind.'[9]

Lord John Russell, the most forward of the pro-Irish section of the cabinet, agreed with O'Connell. A year later, when a tithe bill was introduced with no mention of lay appropriation, he announced, without warning his colleagues of his intention (though they knew his mind) that it was his opinion that 'the revenues of the Church of Ireland were larger than necessary for the religious and moral instruction of the persons belonging to the Church and for the stability of the Church itself'.[10] That declaration was the knell of Whig unity. Stanley, Sir James Graham, the Earl of Ripon and the Duke of Richmond resigned from the cabinet. Two months later, in July, the damning revelation that the government had negotiated with O'Connell when it was deciding whether to renew the coercion bill led, after a series of disclosures embarrassing to ministers, to the retirement of Lord Grey, who was succeeded as prime minister by Lord Melbourne. For all their efforts to come to grips with an aspect of the Irish question, the Whigs had managed to alienate the Irish Radicals, arm the Conservative opposition and split their own party. They had also emboldened the king. In November, unwilling to suffer Lord John Russell as leader of the government in the House of Commons, William IV despatched the Whigs and brought Peel and the Conservatives into office.

Peel's arrival at Downing Street, and substantial Conservative gains at the elections held early in 1835, placed the Whigs in a difficulty. They had no desire to embrace the Radical programme, in which the secret ballot and triennial parliaments were leading elements, nor to make unified cause with O'Connell and the Irish nationalists. Yet a fragmented opposition would be unable to dislodge the minority Conservative administration. They therefore stifled some of their aristocratic pride and at a famous meeting at Lichfield House in February accepted the necessity of a semi-formal alliance with the Radicals and the O'Connellites in order to bring Peel down. The 'Lichfield House compact', as it became known, did not signify a reconstruction of the left of British politics (though for the duration of Melbourne's prime ministership the Radicals and the Irish Brigade veiled their separateness); it did not merge Whiggery and Radicalism in a new Liberal Party.[11] It was, however, successful in its immediate object. After suffering a series of defeats in the House of Commons Peel was forced out of office in April and William IV had no choice but to take back the Whigs.

For the next six years Melbourne's government availed itself of Conservative strength in both Houses to foil the designs of the Radicals.[12] Yet, because the two main parties, especially after further Conservative gains at the 1837 elections, were nearly evenly balanced in the House of Commons, the Whigs were, by themselves, in a minority; they therefore appeared to be ruled by their Irish and Radical tail. Or it was, at least, profitable for the Conservatives to present them in that light. Church matters continued to occupy the central place in parliamentary politics. Melbourne's government presided over some useful reforms which went part of the way towards meeting the Dissenters' demands: a Dissenters' marriage act (which allowed Nonconformists to be married outside an Anglican church, in special circumstances by a civil ceremony), a tithe commutation act and an act enabling London University (which, unlike Oxford and Cambridge, had since its founding in 1825 applied no religious test for the admission of undergraduates) to grant degrees. Those three acts became law in 1836. Two significant failures were the defeat of a Church rates bill in 1837 (the most vexing of the 'injustices' imposed on Dissenters was the requirement to support the established Church by the payment of a local Church rate) and the defeat of an education bill in 1839. The latter would have placed Anglican and Nonconformist schools on a more or less equal footing and laid the foundation of a national system of state education to replace the existing system in which the several religious denominations provided for the education of their own. The howls of protest which the bill raised from Anglican clergymen were expected. At the 1837 elections the country had been sharply divided along religious lines, Nonconformity lending powerful support to the Whigs and the established clergy entering the fray directly and making an 'unprecedented canvass' of electors.[13]

Peel was a stout and shrewd defender of the Church. The one lasting achievement of his brief ministry of 1834–35 was the establishment of the Ecclesiastical Commission, a body of lay and clerical members whose purpose was to correct the undeniable abuses in Church administration – inequality of income from see to see, inadequate payment of the inferior clergy, pluralism and absenteeism – which weakened the Church's ability to stand up to the fire from its enemies. Peel would have the Church reform itself; he would not have it succumb to equal status in law with the Dissenting sects. Hence his implacable opposition to the Whigs' initiative in education.

> Education is the great question to which the public attention should be called. We are to have agitation on that now. It was tried on Church Rates – that failed. It was tried on appropriation of Church Revenue – that failed. ... Now the trial is to be made with education, excluding the direct intervention of the National Church ... there is an end of the Church, and probably an end of any religious feeling at all ultimately.[14]

The Whigs failed to deliver to the Dissenters the redress of their most deeply felt grievances. They failed to push forward the constitutional programme of the Radicals. Yet it is doubtful whether more boldness, a more uncompromisingly radical engagement, would have improved their performance at the 1841 elections. Towards the end of Melbourne's government they did take up the question of the corn laws and, by proposing to replace the existing sliding scale of high tariffs on the import of corn by a small, fixed duty, made an appeal to the urban, manufacturing constituencies. But the alarm which the proposal raised in the counties and the small, rural boroughs outweighed any advantage the issue brought them elsewhere. The threat to the Whigs came from a revived Conservatism, not a disappointed Radicalism. Radicalism was too fragmented and too weakly represented in parliament to inflict damage on a Whig government which failed to meet its aspirations. Disappointed the Dissenters may have been, but they could hardly turn to the Conservatives in their anger. The Dissenters' Parliamentary Committee, formed in 1835 to counter the emergency of a Conservative government, worked for the rest of the decade to support Whig against Conservative parliamentary candidates.[15] Defeat in 1841 was not the result of the Whigs' failure to be sufficiently radical; it was the result of their being sufficiently closely tied to their Irish and Radical friends for the Conservatives to profit from representing them as the enemies of the Church and the constitution.

When he entered the Lichfield compact O'Connell agreed to abandon the agitation for the repeal of the union, to test whether the just government of Ireland from England were possible. The hopes which he placed in Lord Melbourne and, more especially, Lord John Russell were not entirely dupes. Against a Tory House of Lords – which emasculated a bill to place the oligarchic, Orange municipal corporations on a basis similar to the rate-payers' franchise introduced into English corporations by a Whig act of 1835 – it proved difficult to make much legislative impact on Ireland's problems. But for six years Ireland was governed peacefully; the administration of the country from Dublin Castle ceased to be exclusively Orange; and juries were no longer packed with Protestants. Fair-mindedness cost the Whigs dear. For six years they were subjected to abuse, frequently strident, from anti-Catholic sections of the English population. 'Protestantism', Sir James Graham, the ex-Whig who was rising rapidly in Conservative inner counsels, wrote in 1839, 'is the only weapon with which we can encounter Republicanism'.[16] Anti-Irish feeling in England had been growing since Waterloo as Irish immigrants, their numbers swelling yearly, sought work in English towns and the west of Scotland and, being driven to live in the new industrial slums, working in unskilled trades or failing to find work at all, gained a reputation for drunken behaviour and violence, as well as earning contempt for adding to the burden of the poor rate, depressing wages and serving as strike-breakers.[17] So racial antagonism mixed itself with the religious antipathy. The Conservative press relentlessly portrayed Melbourne and his colleagues as traitors to their country. Who, the *Times* asked in 1837, wrote Queen Victoria's first speech from the throne? The answer was savage.

> No other than Lord MELBOURNE, the Whig slave of the Radical, Joseph Hume, and of the anti-Saxon Papist, O'CONNELL – the same Lord MELBOURNE, who has for these last two years and more been levying open war against, or trickily undermining, the ancient laws, the fundamental institutions, and the Protestant monarchy of Great Britain. . . . Has this Whig–Radical 'Ethiopian' changed his skin? – this 'leper' of Popery 'his spots'?[18]

There is little doubt that by 1841 the Whig administration, after a decade in office, was showing signs of strain. Its new poor law, one of its greatest achievements, had brought Whiggery into disodour in the north, where the workhouses were nicknamed 'Bastilles'; the government had handled rebellion in Canada maladroitly and, by its ungracious treatment of Lord Durham, sent overseas to restore order to the colony, offended large sections of the population to whom he became affectionately known as 'Radical Jack'; unemployment and manufacturing depression, deepening every year after 1838, had contributed to what the opposition called financial mismanagement, chiefly the government's inability to balance the national budget. 'The country preferred an Income Tax from Peel to one more deficit from Baring', G. M. Young wrote;[19] but the Conservatives who swallowed the income tax from Peel in 1842 would, in opposition, have fought to the death to prevent the Whigs from foisting it on them. It helped the Conservatives to have in Peel a leader of acknowledged and widely admired financial and parliamentary gifts, a man who gave the air of being in control of events, whereas Lord Melbourne appeared to be at their mercy. Peel was credited with having, as the Tamworth manifesto had promised, rebuilt from the ashes of dispirited Toryism a modern, moderate, efficient Conservative Party. But the truth was that the ultras in Peel's party were as powerful as ever: the 319 opposition members returned at the 1837 elections were classified by the *Annual Register* as 80 Conservatives, 139 Tories and 100 ultra Tories. In those places where the Conservatives might have expected to recapture ground lost in the extraordinary circumstances of 1830 to 1832 – the shires and the small, agricultural boroughs – they did so. The 1841 election result marked a restoration, not a revolution.

John Croker, the political writer for the Tory *Quarterly Review*, believed that at the elections of 1841 everything turned on Peel's name. 'Every Conservative candidate professed himself in plain words to be Sir Robert Peel's man, and on that ground was elected.'[20] Some modern historians have endorsed Croker's verdict. Professor Gash gives almost the entire credit for the Conservative victory to Peel.

> He addressed himself repeatedly to the professional, mercantile and industrial middle classes. He sought to convince them, that, supporters of the Reform Act though they might have been, their

duty was now to combine with the Conservative party in maintaining peace, order and the prosperous evolution of society; and that in turn the Conservative party stood for the defence not merely of the landed aristocracy but of the interests of the solid middle classes of early-Victorian Britain. Two favourite themes, seen for example in his city speech of 1835, the Glasgow civic banquet in 1837, and at the Merchant Taylors Hall dinner of 1838, were the interdependence of industry, commerce and agriculture, and the continuity of British political life and institutions which had shaped the character of the British people. . . . The son of a cotton-manufacturer himself, he tried to effect the political amalgam of classes and interests of which his own family was an example. The electoral success in the urban constituencies which, added to the more predictable victories in the counties, provided the majority of 1841, were a practical reward for all that he had worked for in the previous decade.[21]

Peel, indeed, on several occasions such as those that Professor Gash cites wooed the urban well-to-do with carefully prepared speeches. But in parliament and in his private correspondence he gave little sign that his opinions and attitudes separated him from the Anglicanism and protectionism of his followers. The electoral power of his name and reputation, too, has been exaggerated. It is almost beyond question that the two great issues which swayed Conservative voters in 1841 were the defence of agricultural protection against the Whigs' readiness to tamper with the corn laws and the defence of the Church against the designs of the Dissenters and the Irish Roman Catholics. In the new manufacturing towns, and even in some of the older commercial strongholds, Whiggery remained predominant. The large Conservative majority was won, above all, in the English counties and the small English towns, where the religious issue and the tariff issue damaged the Whigs.[22] The swing of the pendulum brought to Downing Street a prime minister of a new kind – the first true representative of the new age of blue books, royal commissions and select committees, the age of statistics, not rhetoric – but he stood at the head of a party whose members retained the attitudes and assumptions of a dying world.

5

PEEL AND THE NEW CONSERVATISM

The government which Sir Robert Peel formed in the autumn of 1841 took office supported by a party which represented, above all, English agriculture and the Church of England. It is true that Conservative candidates in two-member boroughs with an electorate greater than 1,000 polled a larger share of the vote in 1841 than they had in previous elections; but in the large industrial towns and cities the Conservatives won no more seats than they had in 1835 or 1837. In Scotland and Ireland they were in a minority. By far the most telling statistic of the 1841 returns was that in the English and Welsh counties the Conservatives had an advantage of 137 seats to 22 over the opposition: the heart of Conservative support, the core of its majority (which was somewhere between 76 and 90) lay in the Anglican, protectionist shires.[1] The election results continued a trend which had begun inside the House of Commons itself. In the nine years of Whig government after 1832 defectors from the pro-government benches had swelled the Conservative ranks, and of the 58 'reformers' who crossed the floor of the House of Commons to join the opposition, 54 represented English constituencies.

Much Conservative rhetoric in the 1830s had been directed at the Radicals' destructive designs on the constitution. The Tories had spoken, as they had ever since the days of the younger Pitt, as the Church-and-King party. The difficulty for Peel and his government was that by 1841 constitutional disputes had lost much of their zest. The attack on the Church had been deflected; the Radical Party in parliament was dormant; and although Chartism had a radical political programme – the six points of the Charter were all demands for constitutional reform – much of its force derived from the economic hardship suffered by the mass of the population and many of its supporters were drawn to the movement, not by their abiding interest in constitutional radicalism, but by their participation in the campaigns to repeal the new poor law of 1834 and to institute a ten-hour working day in the textile factories.

Chartism and the Anti-Corn Law League were born in 1838, the year in which the economy turned sharply downwards, the prelude to the 'hungry forties'. For the next five years the economic recession deepened: the year 1842, the first full year of Peel's prime ministership, was one of the most distressed years of the century. The signposts were high unemployment, falling wages, rising food prices and diminishing manufacturing profits. The underlying cause of the crisis was not markedly different from that which had produced similar effects in the years immediately after Waterloo: markets were not expanding quickly enough to absorb the increase in production to which the early industrial revolution had given rise. The home market was depressed and foreign markets were either not large enough (in the undeveloping countries of the empire) or were unwilling (in the developing countries of Europe) to supply the deficiency in domestic purchasing power.[2] The crisis of early industrial capitalism was not new; but there was a difference between 1816 and 1841. The difference was that Peel believed wholeheartedly, as Lord Liverpool had believed only half-heartedly, that economic distress could be, and should be, alleviated by executive policy, that the population had the right to look to government and parliament to provide the framework for economic expansion. In this general view Peel had the backing of influential members of his cabinet, especially Sir James Graham, the home secretary, and the Earl of Ripon, strategically placed as president of the Board of Trade. Ripon, whose successful trade-freeing budgets of the mid-1820s had gained him the nickname, 'Prosperity Robinson', said to Graham on the eve of their coming into office that the fate of a Conservative administration rested on its taking 'an enlarged view of what the actual condition of society demands'.[3]

That prognosis carried a danger for the Conservatives. The government backbenches were crowded with country squires unused to enlarged views, men who believed that the government's overriding duties were to maintain the privileges of the Church of England and defend the supremacy of the landed class. Peel had no wish to injure either the Church or the land. But he thought that neither could be made safe unless the class antagonisms of which Chartism and the Anti-Corn Law League were the visible expressions were dissipated in prosperity. He was at the head of a government which, for the first time in British history, rested on the votes of a single-party majority in the House of Commons. Yet he trusted that party, and the opinions which it held, so little, that within two weeks of forming his administration he took the trouble to warn the party, in a famous speech to the House of Commons, that he would not be induced by 'considerations of mere political support' to hold office 'by a servile tenure which would compel me to be the instrument of carrying other men's opinions into effect'.[4] In the end the majority of his party was unable to forgive him precisely for carrying other men's opinions into effect, for catching the Whigs bathing, as Disraeli put it, and running off with their clothes. From 1841 to 1846 the parliamentary battle that mattered was the one that took place within the Conservative Party. The Whig Party, worn out by a decade in government, rescued Peel's legislation from Conservative opposition; as an opposition itself it was of little significance.

No failure had so dogged the Whigs in the late 1830s as their inability to balance the budget. The Conservatives had readily seized upon that failure as the primary mark of Whig incompetence. Peel's first task was therefore to demonstrate the superiority of Conservative over Whig financial management. It was a challenge he was the more eager to accept because the immediate object of overcoming the chronic deficit fitted well with his long-term strategy to raise the level of manufacturing prosperity in the country. The budget of 1842 effectively ended the deficit by reintroducing the income and property tax (at the rate of threepence in the pound). And it went further. The income tax, by creating a surplus, enabled Peel to reduce the duties on a wide range of imported goods and to make a downwards revision of the sliding scale of corn duties (which had stood unaltered since 1828), lowering the maximum duty on imported wheat from 50s 8d to 20s. Any reduction in the corn duties was unwelcome to some Conservatives, but the imposition of an income tax was a touchier matter. The tax had been levied for the first time in British history by the younger Pitt during the early years of the war against France and it had been repealed in the first year of peace. The notion had thus entered the political stock-in-trade of the country that it was a harsh and inquisitorial expedient justifiable only by the heavy financial burdens of war-making. Peel was careful to present the restoration of the tax as a temporary measure, necessary to overcome the deficit only for so long as it took for the increased consumption which he expected to flow from tariff reductions to provide additional revenue to the exchequer. The Conservative backbenchers, unwilling to embarrass the government in its infancy and reassured by Peel's statement that to get rid of the corn laws would not alleviate urban distress but simply add rural poverty to it, offered scant resistance to the budget. Nine Conservatives voted against the new sliding scale and two against the income tax.

As early as 1842, even so, there was evidence that Peel could not rely on his party to follow blindly wherever he led them. The customs bill included a clause to abolish the prohibition on the import of foreign beef into the country and to replace it with a duty of £1 per head of cattle: 86 Conservatives (56 of them members for English counties) voted against the change, which was nevertheless carried decisively. Had the Conservative Party as a whole understood the direction in which Peel's mind was travelling, the misgivings of the agriculturalists might have manifested themselves more uninhibitedly. There is no doubt that Peel looked upon the income tax, not simply as a mechanical means of balancing the budget, but as an instrument to gain a wider social and economic objective. Reducing prices by lowering tariffs and relieving the burden of taxation on the less well-off by shifting taxation away from indirect and towards more direct taxation were measures intended to increase the purchasing power of the consumer. 'The danger', Peel said to a colleague, 'is not low price from the tariff, but low price from inability to consume.'[5] Publicly he was bold enough to claim in the House of Commons that all parties were now agreed on the general principle of free trade and on the general rule of buying in the cheapest markets overseas and selling in the dearest. But the implications of the statement were somewhat clouded by his insistence that the growers of wheat (whose crops were more expensively produced than those abroad) were entitled, because they bore special burdens such as the payment of the land tax, to the compensatory protection afforded them by the corn laws. Murmers of disapproval were nevertheless heard in the constituencies and the outward docility of the party in the House of Commons reflected the grudging attitude expressed by one Tory paper, that it was better for the agriculturalists to accept with what grace they could muster measures from 'a friendly government avowedly desirous of affording them the utmost possible extent of protection' rather than to trust to the mercies of the opposite party, which repudiated the very principle of protection.[6]

Peel asked for a fair trial for his system (the income tax had a life of three years); the agriculturalists on the backbenches looked upon the 1842 sliding scale as a settlement of the tariff issue. There is no evidence that Peel acknowledged to himself that the next step would have to be, as Sir James Graham suggested at the end of the year, a step to 'an open trade';[7] but nor can it be said that he was startled or alarmed by Graham's opinion. He had, as a modern historian has described it, presented the new sliding scale with 'a wonderful equivocation which left him free to move backwards to protection or forwards to free trade'.[8] Financial questions did not, as it turned out, occupy a prominent place in parliamentary debates for the following three years. Outside parliament, however, the Anti-Corn Law League was gathering strength and extending its recruiting activities beyond the manufacturing centres into the shires. A series of by-election successes for the League included a near-victory in the rural, cathedral town of Salisbury, where in 1843 its candidate polled 45 per cent of the vote. In the House of Commons, too, keen-eyed observers did not fail to notice that the speeches of Richard Cobden, the leader of the League and an accomplished orator, did not draw from Peel stout rebuttals in the defence of the corn laws. And in 1843 the founding of the first of the Protection Societies in the English counties (a movement which spread rapidly enough for the emergence by 1844 of what was popularly called the Anti-League)[9] presaged an intensification of the animosity between town and country, manufacturing industry and agriculture, which it was Peel's primary purpose to dilute.

The 1844 session of parliament began with an announcement from Peel, in the debate on the address to the throne, that his government did not contemplate, and had never contemplated, any change in the existing corn laws. And although only a few weeks later he turned to his cabinet colleague, Sidney Herbert, after a powerful free-trade speech from Cobden, and whispered, 'you must answer this, for I cannot', the statement was technically accurate. No proposal to alter the law had been laid before the cabinet for discussion. But the coldness of the statement, combined with Peel's silence in the face of Cobden's arguments, kindled disquiet among the backbenchers. Whether partly for that reason or entirely independent of it, the Conservative rank-and-file displayed in 1844 a readiness to rebel against the policy of the government on two important occasions: the first, a bill to reduce the number of hours that children might be employed in the textile mills, and the second, later in the session, a bill to reduce the duty on the import of free-grown foreign sugar (excluding, that is, sugar grown in slave nations) in order to supplement the ever-diminishing supply of sugar coming from the Caribbean colonies, which for many years had enjoyed a near-monopoly of the trade.

Sugar and cotton were key products in the British economy. The textile trade supplied five-sixths of the country's total exports and sugar, a staple ingredient in the national diet and an important item in the ordinary family's cost of living, was one of the most lucrative sources of the revenue which the exchequer gained from import duties. It cannot be said, therefore, that the Conservative backbenchers who deserted the government lobbies were merely letting off steam on minor issues which had little significance in themselves; nor that Peel and his ministers, in standing firm against the dissidents, were guilty of a misjudgement of priorities.

The factory bill proposed to raise the age limit at which children might be employed from eight to nine; and it sought to restrict the number of working hours for children to six-and-a-half a day. The bill left untouched the provision of the existing act (passed in 1833) that limited the number of hours for women and young persons to twelve and it ignored the campaign in the country for a ten-hour day for all adults. Lord Ashley (better known to posterity by his later title, the Earl of Shaftesbury), an evangelical Protestant and an eminent member of the paternalist wing of the Conservative Party which supported humanitarian causes and had given the ten-hours agitation a number of leaders, brought in an amendment to reduce the number of hours for women and young persons to ten. The Peelite wing of the party, having drunk deep from the well of *laisser-faire*, classical economics, was never eager to interfere in the free operation of the market, in the contractual relationship between master and man, or between capital and labour. An exception was made for children; but everyone knew that to enforce a ten-hour day for women and young persons was, in fact, because of the large number of such persons employed in the mills, to introduce it for adult men as well. The mills would not stay open after half the work force had gone home for the day. There was also general agreement (though sharp disagreement about how much) that wages would fall if hours were reduced. Peel thought it wrong to reduce wages at the very time when the government, by upholding the corn laws against the manufacturers and the Anti-Corn Law League, was helping to sustain price levels of bread. He also thought it wrong, just at the time when the prosperity of manufacturing industry was the key to national economic revival, to act in any way that might injure productivity in the textile industry.

The motives which led nearly a third of the Conservative

Party to take Ashley's side against the cabinet were mixed. There had always been a paternalist, 'Tory Radical' element in the party, an element which in the 1830s had joined the protest against the 1834 poor law and, on behalf of the ten-hours campaign principally, had even made electoral alliance with the Chartists in a few constituencies. It is not, perhaps, surprising that men who passed their lives in the closely-knit agricultural community, with its traditional emphasis on landlords' duties as well as rights and its genuine belief (however much honoured in the breach) in the ties of mutual responsibility that bound men of one class to men of another, men, in addition, who knew little from direct observation of life in the industrial towns, should have had little sympathy with the highly individualistic social values of the new political economy. And it is probably true that a number of them, alarmed at the growth of the Anti-Corn Law League and vexed by its agents' intrusions into the countryside, were happy to beat the manufacturers and their free-trade allies with any stick. 'A greaty body of the agricultural members,' Peel informed the queen after Ashley's amendment was carried against the government, 'partly out of hostility to the Anti-Corn Law League, partly from the influence of humane feelings, not foreseeing the certain consequences as to the Corn Laws of new restrictions upon labour, voted against the Government.'[10]

The number of Tory rebels was 95. A few months later 62 Conservatives, many of whom had also supported Ashley, voted for the amendment to the government's sugar bill introduced by Philip Miles, the Conservative member for Bristol (a port having strong links with the sugar trade). Miles's amendment had the effect of restoring to the colonial planters some of the preferential tariff advantage over foreign producers that the bill proposed to eliminate. Once again the combination of opposition and rebel Conservative votes was sufficiently strong to defeat the government. On both occasions, however, Peel won the day in the end by prevailing upon the House of Commons to reverse its vote a few nights later. Enough Conservative rebels, brought into line by Peel's threat to resign, either abstained or changed their votes to give the government's original proposals narrow majorities.

Whether permanent damage was done to the government by those two episodes is a question open to argument. Francis Bonham reported to Peel during the second crisis that the number of Conservatives who were actually 'inimical' to the government was no more than twenty and that even fewer were prepared to drive the government from office and let in the Whigs.[11] On the other hand, Conservative backbenchers were angry with Peel for insisting on getting his own way against the declared will of the legislature; and large numbers of those Conservatives who voted against him in 1844 also voted against him in the much larger and more serious Tory rebellion against the Maynooth bill in 1845 and in the culminating Conservative crisis over the corn laws in 1846.[12] A rift was developing in the party and disloyalty is always easier the second time. As Professor Conacher has written, 'explosions such as that which occurred in the Conservative Party in 1846 do not come completely out of the blue'.[13]

What the two crises revealed was a different attitude towards party and its relation to the executive held by backbenchers, on the one side, and the cabinet, on the other. It was difficult for members of parliament who cherished the tradition of 'independence' to allow that the Houses of Parliament had become, as one country gentleman phrased it, 'mere places of registration of the laws proposed by the Ministers of the Crown'.[14] Yet if party were to replace the crown as the bedrock of ministerial stability – that is, if the logic of reform and the growth of the party system was to be followed out – the executive needed to know that it could rely on the support of party. Peel was somewhat graceless in his handling of the 1844 disputes: in the middle of each he called the parliamentary party together, not to discuss the question or listen to the arguments of the dissidents, but simply to announce that the government would resign if the House of Commons persisted in its delinquency. It was a continuing difficulty in the Conservative Party that Peel, by his aloofness from his backbenchers, was unable to inspire their affection. But he was right to insist, against those who argued that defeats on particular bills did not imply a withdrawal of general confidence, that declarations of general confidence could not compensate for the loss of authority sustained by a government which was unable to carry its practical legislation through parliament and which was compelled to witness the transfer of 'the duties of Government, so far as legislation is concerned, to parties wholly irresponsible and much less informed than Ministers are or ought to be'.[15]

Tension between the legislature and the executive is an inescapable ingredient of the parliamentary system. Party serves to prevent that tension from emasculating the executive. It can do so, however, only when a more or less explicit common accord exists between the government and its parliamentary followers. In the early days of party that common accord was difficult to establish because of the absence of a declared programme or party manifesto. It may be true that in 1841 every Conservative candidate declared himself to be 'Peel's man'; what was not clear was what being Peel's man entailed. Peel believed that the Conservative Party 'stood in the first place for strong executive government as the rock on which all else must stand'.[16] His doctrine (as every government's tends to be) was 'men, not measures'. The doctrine was not always easy for backbenchers to swallow. For one thing, they had to face pressure from their constituents' opinions. In 1842, when Peel managed to get his tariff changes accepted with little overt opposition, warning bells were sounded: Philip Pusey, the influential Conservative member of parliament for Berkshire, in the heart of agricultural England, called upon his colleagues on the backbenches to look to measures, not men, and to consider that 'it is not our own property we are dealing with, but that of our constituents'.[17]

Lord Salisbury, the Conservative prime minister during the last years of the 19th century, was fond of repeating the dictum that the only truly powerful influences upon men, acting in a mass, were hunger and religion. In the 1840s hunger played its part in the two national campaigns for the Charter and the repeal of the corn laws. The influence of religion, seemingly dormant for much of the 18th century (when religious 'enthusiasm' was distinctly unfashionable), but outwardly and inwardly revived by the preaching of the Methodists and the Evangelicals, was pervasive in early Victorian life and politics. Evangelical

71

Anglicanism lent leaders like Ashley to the anti-poor law and ten hours agitations; Dissent added sinew to the Anti-Corn Law League's denunciations of the rural dominance of parson and squire (League speakers frequently made a connection between the payment of tithes by farmers to the Church and the high cost of bread); and in Ireland land hunger and the Roman Catholic faith brought priest and people together in the war against Protestant, imperial England.

Ireland posed a direct threat to Peel's government. Daniel O'Connell's movement for the repeal of the union, which had been suspended during Lord Melbourne's administration, was revived as soon as the Conservatives came into office and the large crowds which gathered at the 'monster' outdoor meetings of 1842 and 1843 masked the fact, which contemporaries cannot be blamed for failing to see, that O'Connell's declining powers and strict legalism were opening the way to fissures in the nationalist movement, fissures that were to debilitate Irish nationalism for a generation. To Peel's own supporters what appeared evident was that the government was zealous in its efforts to conciliate Irish Catholicism and lukewarm in its defence of the established Church.[18] Peel consistently refused to answer appeals for state funds to assist the programme of Church extension, especially in the rapidly growing industrial towns whose populations were at risk of being left untouched by the Gospels. He preferred to leave it to the Ecclesiastical Commission to redistribute the ample revenues of the Church and provide for the cure of the urban poor from its own resources. Excitable Churchmen began to wonder if they alone were friendless in high places. Dissent gained a victory over them in 1843, when the clauses in Sir James Graham's factory bill which gave control over the education of children working in factories to the established Church were withdrawn in the face of vociferous protests from the sects. (The clauses were not restored in the bill which became law a year later.) The government was busy, too, sending what Disraeli called 'messages of peace' to the Irish Catholics. The charitable bequests act of 1844 made it easier for persons to make gifts of land or money to the Roman Catholic Church in Ireland. Peel also attempted, with only limited success, to continue the Whig practice of distributing Irish patronage fairly among Protestants and Roman Catholics, while his appointment of the Devon Commission to inquire into the conditions of land tenure in Ireland hinted at a readiness to enhance the status and improve the material welfare of the Catholic tenantry and weaken the social and economic ascendancy of the Protestant landowners. Within England itself anti-Catholic sentiment had been stirred by the Romish tendency of the Oxford Movement, initiated by the Reverend John Henry Newman in 1833. Exquisitely intellectual though they may have been, and confined to the more erudite reaches of the Church, the teachings of the Tractarians (the name derived from the series of tracts in which Newman and his allies published their opinions), that in a liberal age the Church stood to lose more than it gained by its established link with the state (which was bound to be broadminded or 'latitudinarian' in its views on Church dogma and discipline) and that an essential harmony existed between the Thirty-Nine Articles of the Church of England and the ancient doctrines of the Roman Church, affronted orthodox Churchmen, especially when, by the mid-1840s, there began a steady trickle of Anglican converts to Rome.

Newman himself announced his conversion in 1845, the very year in which the Conservative Party was torn in two by Peel's decision to place the Roman Catholic seminary at Maynooth, the college in County Kildare at which young men were trained for the Catholic priesthood, on a sound financial basis. The Maynooth bill trebled the college's parliamentary grant (from £9,000 to £26,000 a year) and made the grant permanent, not, as it had been, dependent upon an annual vote of the legislature.[19] It was a small measure, part of the government's policy to develop higher education for Irish Roman Catholics (the charitable bequests act and the foundation of the Queen's Colleges were other items in the policy) and so detach moderate Catholics from the repeal movement. Its practical contribution to the solving of the Irish question was negligible, and for that reason the first historian of the 19th-century Tory Party, writing in 1886, described the furore which it raised as 'one of the most pitiful incidents in the whole history of Toryism'.[20] On the bill's second reading the Conservative Party in the House of Commons split 159 in favour and 147 against; on the third reading the 149 Conservatives who voted against the bill actually outnumbered by one the number of its Conservative supporters. Almost the entire Whig Party voted in favour of the bill.

No doubt those divisions reflected a primitive intolerance of Catholicism in sections of the Conservative Party both inside and outside parliament. Public expressions of horror greeted Peel's statement, in announcing the government's intention, that the government did 'not propose to accompany that increased vote [in the grant] by any regulations in respect of the doctrines and disciplines of the Church of Rome, that can diminish the grace and favour of the grant'.[21] But the great opposition to the bill which was mounted in the country rested on something more than native prejudice. It was grounded in deeply-held convictions about the proper relationships which ought to exist between the state and religion. The petitions against the bill that rained upon the House of Commons – 2,400 of them by the time that the debate on the second reading began – came in about equal proportions from the Anglican and Dissenting parts of the population, each of which resented any measure of state support for Roman Catholicism, though not for the identical reasons. Anglicans believed in the religious purpose and office of the state: the state had a *conscience* in the matter of religion and could propagate and establish only that one denomination of Christianity where its conscience resided. Moreover, the state had, in Churchmen's eyes, no business giving aid and comfort to a church whose members owed their first loyalty to the Vatican and were therefore tainted with at least the suspicion of disloyalty to the crown. The Dissenters, especially the Baptists and Independents, believed in the separation of Church and state and their new political movement, the Anti-State Church Association (known after 1853 as the Liberation Society), had been formed a year earlier to campaign not only for the abolition of Church rates, but for the disestablishment of the Church itself.[22] For some time English politicians had been exercising themselves to devise a means of detaching the Irish priesthood from nationalist agitation: one repeated suggestion was the state endowment of the Roman Catholic clergy, by which means it was thought that priests might be rendered less dependent on their flock and more tied to the crown. To both Dissenter and Churchmen, therefore, the Maynooth grant, paltry in itself, could be interpreted as a small, but dangerous, step towards the establishment – or the 'concurrent endowment' – of the Roman Church in Ireland. A number of opposition speakers in the debates expressed the hope that the increased grant would indeed be the precursor of other similar, and more far-reaching, changes. The Central Anti-Maynooth Committee was partly successful in forging an unholy alliance between the Dissenting voluntarists and the Anglican defenders of the establishment throughout the empire,[23] but Peel was right to dismiss the possibility of lasting cooperation or effective electoral compact between the uneasy allies. At seventeen by-elections held between the passing of the Maynooth bill in April 1845 and the opening of the autumn session of parliament that year the government suffered no net loss of seats.

In parliament the bill was carried by comfortable majorities because the Whig opposition, despite the electoral strength which it received from the Dissenters, acted in accordance with its historic attachment to the principle of religious toleration. Whig votes falsified Peel's forecast, made on the eve of the 1845 session, that the Maynooth issue would 'very probably be fatal to the Government'.[24] Yet damage had been done to the Conservative Party. Within its ranks a core of opposition to Peel and the liberal direction of his government was forming itself. Half of the rebels on the factory bill a year earlier also voted against the Maynooth grant; only 11 of them voted for it. And of the 162 Conservatives who voted against the Maynooth bill at one of its stages through the House of Commons only 20 were to vote for the repeal of the corn laws in the following year; 133 of them were to vote against repeal. Whether Peel was, as the violently anti-Catholic Lord Ashley wrote in his diary, 'the most unpopular head of a party that ever existed',[25] he had forfeited much Conservative esteem, not least by stirring memories of his 'betrayal' of 1829. Sir James Graham knew that the party was 'shivered and angry' and that the government had 'lost the slight hold which we ever possessed over the hearts and kind feelings of our followers'.[26] Graham habitually looked on the dark side of things, but it was ominous for the government that the Conservative dissidents had discovered in 1845 a new spokesman. It would be untrue to suggest that Disraeli took possession of their hearts and feelings; many of them found the ferocity of his sarcasm distasteful. But they applauded his theme. His speech in opposition to the Maynooth bill, one of the most savage, and skilfully savage, attacks ever delivered by an English member of parliament against the leader of his own party, raised the dispute far beyond the details of the bill itself. At issue was the place of party, and the proper use of party, in a parliamentary constitution.

This bill brings affairs to a crisis; the question is not to be decided on its merits; it is to be decided on the fact – who are the men who bring it forward? If you are to have a popular Government, if you are to have a Parliamentary Administration, the conditions antecedent are, that you have a Government which declares the principles upon which its policy is founded, and then you can have on them the wholesome check of a constitutional Opposition. What have we got instead? Something has risen up in this country as fatal in the political world as it has been in the landed world of Ireland – we have a great Parliamentary middleman. It is well known what a middleman is; he is a man who bamboozles one party, and plunders the other, till, having obtained a position to which he is not entitled, he cries out, 'Let us have no party questions, but fixity of tenure.' I want to have a Commission issued to inquire into the tenure by which Downing Street is held. . . . Let us in this House re-echo that which I believe to be the sovereign sentiment of this country; let us tell persons in high places that cunning is not caution, and that habitual perfidy is not high policy of state. On that ground we may all join. Let us bring back to this House that which it has for so long a time past been without – the legitimate influence and salutary check of a constitutional opposition. That is what the country requires, what the country looks for. Let us do it at once in the only way in which it can be done, by dethroning this dynasty of deception, by putting to an end the intolerable yoke of official despotism and Parliamentary imposture.[27]

6

FREE TRADE AND ITS AFTERMATH

By the mid-1840s the case for free trade was, in the minds of political economists and those politicians who looked upon themselves as progressive, becoming almost unanswerable. Peel himself had been intellectually a free-trader, in an abstract sense, for some time, probably since as far back as the 1820s,[1] and he might have moved more quickly, in office after 1841, towards giving effect to his opinions had he not been held back by the political restraints which his position at the head of the Conservative Party and his own, frequently enunciated defence of the corn laws placed upon his freedom of action. After the sweeping tariff reductions included in the 1845 budget (more extensive than those of 1842), the high duty on corn took on the appearance of an anomaly in the country's financial system, and Peel was probably speaking the truth when he told Prince Albert in December 1845 that his intention had been to prepare the country gradually for a change in policy and to contest the elections which were due in two years' time on a platform of free trade in corn. He meant thereby to deprive the Whigs of the electoral advantage to be gained from the cry of 'cheap bread' and so avert an election battle that would heighten class tensions and exacerbate whatever ill-feelings existed between urban manufacturers and rural growers. Postponing the decision would also enable him to take the members of his party into his confidence and slowly 'educate' them in the wisdom of classical economics.

But it is the lot of politicians to see their intentions frustrated by events. The potato blight in Ireland, of which news began to reach the cabinet in late August, news that became blacker by the week as a rainy summer gave way to a rainy autumn, raised the spectre of famine. The blight was prevalent throughout Europe and a poor harvest generally, including grain crops, was certain to raise food prices. How, then, were Englishmen to be asked to support famine relief in Ireland and at the same time continue to pay for protection in high wheat prices? Whether the graduated scale of duties voted by parliament in 1828 and revised in 1842 had materially affected the price of bread remains a question to which historians are unable to give a conclusive answer (there is less doubt about the scale's failure to achieve one of its objects, stability of price in good seasons and bad). Both free-trader and protectionist believed, however, that it had done so and would continue to do so. Although the output of British agriculture since Waterloo had just about kept pace with the increased consumption by an expanding population, few people doubted that, unless it were dramatically increased, Great Britain would, if not in the immediate, nor in the far distant, future, become more and more dependent on foreign sources of supply.[2]

As soon as the reports from Ireland confirmed the imminence of widespread famine (the Irish peasantry lived on a subsistence potato diet and was, for the most part, too poor to buy replacement foods during a potato shortage), Peel and Graham came without hesitation to the conclusion that the days of protected food were over, and there is much point to Professor Gash's remark that 'the instant certainty that famine meant repeal could only have come to men who were already convinced that the corn laws could no longer be defended'.[3] In Peel's mind there was another, urgent reason not to delay. He was ready to announce himself a free-trader; but he had not decided to adopt the urban, middle-class view of politics. He remained a Conservative, intent on upholding the place of the aristocracy in national affairs and fearful that the aristocracy would bring about its own downfall by tying its fortunes to the maintenance of the corn laws. 'The worst ground on which we can *now* fight the battle for institutions – for the just privileges of Monarchy and Landed Aristocracy', he wrote to a Conservative backbencher, 'is on a question of food.'[4] The 'now' was what counted. In 1842 Peel had told John Croker, an unrelenting protectionist, that 'if you had to constitute new societies, you might on moral and social grounds prefer cornfields to cotton factories, an agricultural to a manufacturing population. But our lot is cast and we cannot recede.'[5] Eager to secure the 'just privileges' of the aristocracy, Peel did not wish to hand the initiative to the Anti-Corn Law League, which would undoubtedly exploit to the full the new opportunity which the prospect of famine presented to bolster its crusade against what it unceasingly described as a rapacious and selfish landowning class. Repeal, when it came, was not to be allowed to appear as the prize wrenched from a Conservative government by a conquering League. A long battle with the League, fought while Irish peasants starved, would re-ignite the social tensions which had abated since the dark years of 1838 to 1842. Victory for the League at the end of it would establish a precedent for successful extra-parliamentary agitation; and it would give repeal the colour of a triumph for the industrial bourgeoisie over the forces of reactionary agrarianism. Peel wished to make repeal appear as the symbol of class reconciliation. In the speech at the beginning of the 1846 session of parliament in which he announced his repeal measure one sentence stood out from the rest. It has been much quoted and it deserves to be, for however baldly it contrasted with his reproach of the Whigs in 1841 for 'stirring up society to its foundation and . . . arraying against each other, in bitter discord, classes of the community whose harmony is essential to their own welfare'[6] by dissolving parliament on a cry of cheap bread, it put succinctly the interpretation which Peel wished men to place upon his actions.

> I have thought it consistent with true Conservative policy to promote so much of happiness and contentment among the people that the voice of disaffection should be no longer heard, and that thought of the dissolution of our institutions should be forgotten in the midst of physical enjoyment.[7]

The protectionists on the Conservative benches argued that,

if the Irish famine were the true cause of Peel's actions, he should simply have suspended the corn laws for a period, not got rid of them altogether. Peel believed that that option was not really available: to suspend the tariff would be to acknowledge that it kept up the price of food and encouraged scarcity, an admission which would make it practically impossible, after a period in which men and women had grown accustomed to the benefits of free trade, to return to protection. The explanation was never accepted by the protectionists in the Conservative Party who believed that Peel had used the 'godsend' of the Irish harvest as an excuse to bring forward a long-matured 'secret design'.[8] Croker could not forgive Peel for the 'deception' of attributing his decision to the potato failure[9] and the protectionists in general recognised no force in the explanation, arguing instead that as the sliding scale then stood the duty on corn would have passed away before famine prices were reached. Their suspicion of Peel's motives was deepened when the details of the repeal measure were announced in January: in place of the existing minimum duty of 1s per quarter on the 1842 scale the new terms provided for a minimum duty of 4s for three years, after which the corn laws were to expire. And the protectionists felt vindicated in 1847, when, to meet the reality of famine, parliament agreed to suspend the remedial measure of 1846 in order to let wheat in at 1s per quarter, just as it would have been admitted under the old law.

The cabinet, which met regularly throughout October and November to discuss the crisis, agreed that suspension was impracticable; but Peel and Graham had great difficulty in persuading their colleagues that the necessity of repeal was so invincible as to compel them to desert their principles. Peel put off the day when the cabinet would have to decide until early December, by which time a new element had come into play. Lord John Russell, the leader of the Whigs, published a letter from Edinburgh on 22 November in which he announced his commitment to repeal and called upon the country to join him in the effort to make the government buckle to free-trade pressure. Russell's contribution to the crisis made it highly improbable that the government would be able to make repeal its work without laying itself open to the accusation that it acted, not according to its convictions, but at the dictation of its political opponents. Conservative ministers would be cast in the light of office-greedy time-servers. When, therefore, Lord Stanley and the Duke of Buccleuch, two of the richest landowners in the kingdom, declared at the cabinet meeting of 4 December that they could not with consistency or honour remain in a free-trade government, Peel, despite having brought the rest of his colleagues around, informed the queen of his government's resignation. The queen sent for Russell and asked him to form a government. Russell failed; and Peel came back into office greatly strengthened by the Whigs' inability, or unwillingness, to accept 'the poisoned chalice'.[10] The question had become not so much in what manner the queen's government was to be carried on, as whether it were to be carried on at all. Buccleuch stayed on and Peel prepared to face parliament in January weakened only by the loss of Stanley, a formidable loss, but one softened by Stanley's promise not to speak against the government.

The economic case for free trade, at least as Peel understood it, was that manufacturing exports were essential to the national prosperity and that foreign markets would be unable to absorb goods from Great Britain's workshops unless they earned the money to pay for them by selling grain in the British market. Whether Great Britain yet needed enough foreign grain – the country had only just ceased to be self-sufficient in food – for its imports to be large enough to open up overseas markets in the immediate future was a moot question. But the economic malaise of the post-Waterloo years stemmed, to a large degree, from the failure of markets to expand as rapidly as industrial productivity (although the railway boom of the 1840s gave a great stimulus to the manufacture of iron) and, since neither prevailing economic theory (which accepted the notion of a wages fund, a more or less fixed amount of capital available for distribution as wages) nor employment practices enabled markets to be expanded by increasing the wages and hence the purchasing power of the home consumer, it was assumed by nearly everyone who thought about such matters that recovery would have to be export-led.* To that Peel added the argument that agricultural prosperity was interwoven with manufacturing prosperity, on which it depended more than it did on the corn laws. Landowners were advised to look to the methods of scientific farming propagated by the Agricultural Association (the draining of estates, improved methods of crop rotation and soil enrichment and a shift from arable to livestock farming) to increase their productivity and maintain profitable levels of rent.

The protectionists in the Conservative Party did not accept that analysis of farming's future. They looked at the economic aspects of the free-trade debate from their own vantage point and what they saw was very different from the picture painted by the political economists. Agriculture as a commercial enterprise had never been restored to the heights achieved during the Napoleonic wars, when soaring prices and the dependence on home crops had brought many acres previously unreclaimed into productivity. The average price of wheat in the 1830s and 1840s was barely half what it had been at its wartime peak; and while rental from houses rose by 140 per cent between 1815 and 1845, rental from land increased by only 12 per cent. At the same time the expense of cultivation had increased by about 50 per cent. Farming, the Tory historian and journalist, Archibald Alison, pointed out, was not a thriving business.

We see cultivation everywhere extended, and the most strenuous

---

* It did not serve Peel's purpose to say so, but the importance of foreign markets did not lie entirely in their ability to provide cheap food and take English manufactures. The 19th century was an age of ever-expanding credit and foreign markets were attractive to moneylenders as an extensive field for the profitable business of capital investment. Cobden and the League conjured up images of a world made secure from war by the commercial interdependence of free-trading nations. But in the prospectus of the *Economist*, launched in 1843 as a journal pledged to the repeal of the corn laws, the note of economic imperialism was already to be heard in free-trade arguments that rested more on financial than industrial considerations. The only cure for over-productivity was increased demand (the argument ran) and home demand could not be increased: 'there can be no increased demand without increased markets; and we cannot secure larger markets without an unrestricted power of exchange, and by this means add to our territory of land, as far as productive utility is concerned, the corn fields of Poland, Prussia, and above all, the rich and endless acres of the United States'. (See C. H. Sisson, *The Case of Walter Bagehot*, London, 1972, pp. 102–3.)

efforts made frequently to drain and improve the soil; but we perceive scarcely any traces of these exertions leading to the accumulation of fortunes among their authors. It is painfully evident that these efforts are made, not to accumulate money, but to avert ruin. . . . We often hear of shopkeepers and merchants buying villas in the country to enjoy themselves in summer, but we never hear of farmers buying houses in town for recreation in winter. They do not even acquire small properties in the country.[11]

It irked the farmers, since the low prices which wheat fetched in the 1830s and 1840s made it unconvincing to argue that high prices were keeping down consumption, to be branded by the Anti-Corn Law League as class tyrants, living off a tax levied on the rest of the community. Their reply to the advocates of scientific or 'high' farming was that protected prices and security from overseas competition were essential to enable them to make heavy capital investments in improvement, investments which brought a very slow rate of return. Landowners with little capital could afford to take up improved farming only by mortgaging or selling parts of their estates, thus undermining their efforts to build up and perpetuate their inheritances so that they could, in turn, pass them on to their heirs intact or increased. Land-ownership was not simply a business, organised for profit. It was a way of life. The value of land was as much the status it conferred on its owner as the income it brought him. Many landowners did not accept that Great Britain was irrevocably set on the path that led to an urban, industrial culture. In each year from 1814 to 1846 the parliamentary returns showed that the import of wheat and wheat-flour was below one million quarters, usually far below; home production had kept pace with increased consumption. Archibald Alison calculated that, after setting aside one-half of the arable land of the country for the production of luxury foods, the rest could yield enough corn and potatoes to feed a population of at least 120 million.[12]

The agriculturalists also complained that since lower prices were not matched by reduced rents, farmers were living more and more on their capital, and that since few gentlemen would invest in so insecure a business, arable land would be converted to pasture and England would cease to be self-sufficient in food.

The complaint carried little weight with the free-traders, whose notion of the world economy explicitly included an international division of labour. And even if it were true that England would no longer be able to supply herself with corn, it was not evident that the national diet would suffer from an increased consumption of meat and potatoes. From a foreigner's point of view it was evident that the opposite was true.

> High duties do not produce great crops, nor do low duties necessarily lead to the decline of national agriculture. . . . English agriculture, with comparatively the smallest number of hands, produces the largest crops, and supports by far the greatest number of individuals not agriculturalists. But if the number of agriculturalists is comparatively smaller, and the quantity produced greater than in other places, the capitals must be larger, the mode of cultivation better; knowledge of the business more general; the facilities (for instance, good roads, canals, navigation, etc.) more numerous; it necessarily follows, in a word, that English agriculture, if we take a general view, must be on the whole flourishing, progressive, and more perfect than in any other country in the world. And of this I am thoroughly persuaded; notwithstanding all the lamentations which distress here and there extorts, or which party spirit has often put forward to serve its own ends, but which will hardly serve its turn much longer.[13]

A flourishing agriculture employing fewer and fewer hands was the agriculturalists' nightmare, especially for the tenant farmers, who resisted free trade far more fiercely than the higher ranks of the landed class. Yet an ever-diminishing agricultural population threatened the whole of the landed community. For generations the gentry and yeomanry had looked upon themselves, and been looked upon, as a virtuous and useful class, the repository of the independence of spirit that underlay English freedoms. The independent country gentleman was proud of his place in parliament and jealous of his traditional administrative and legal duties in the locality. He was resentful of agents of the central government like the poor law commissioners, who encroached on his fief. He was bewildered by the world of cotton masters and Chartists. If the 'tide of history' was flowing against him he did not understand why it should, nor did he believe that he was powerless to turn it.

Because the agriculturalists did not accept the *necessity* of repeal, they resented its coming from Peel and a Conservative government, who, they believed, ought to have been restrained by constitutional scruples from turning round on their former statements and giving additional substance to Disraeli's jibe during the Maynooth debates that a Conservative government was an 'organised hypocrisy'. Shorn of economic necessity, the League's campaign against the landed interest appeared to be nothing more than an assault on the social and political status of the aristocracy and gentry. Cobden, though he was born and raised in a small Sussex village[14] and spent only fifteen years of his life in Manchester as a successful calico-printer, said that he and most of the Leaguers had entered upon the fight against the corn laws in 'the belief that we had some distinct class-interest in the question';[15] and John Croker, from the other side of the barricades, argued that prices and wages were merely accidental to the real quarrel: 'the *substance* is the existence of a landed gentry, which has made England what she has been and is; without which no representative government can last; without which there can be no steady mean between democracy and despotism'.[16] The Duke of Richmond took the same line: the League would not stop at ruining the agricultural interest, which was but the first step towards eliminating the influence of the yeomanry and the land and ushering in the radically democratic principles by which they meant to subvert the constitution.[17]

Richmond was the president of the Central Protection Society and since 1843, when the first of the local protection societies had been formed in Essex on the initiative of the tenant farmer, Robert Baker, he had been closely involved in building up the network of such societies throughout the English counties that made up the 'Anti-League'. The general committee of the central society was composed of eighteen members of parliament, all but two of whom were Conservatives, and twenty tenant farmers. Down to December 1845 the society studiously maintained a non-political stance and eschewed any participation in electoral matters. The Conservative government's change of course forced it to alter its policy and for the next few months, while the repeal debates were taking place in parliament, the society applied great pressure on Conservative members of parliament either to oppose the free-trade measure or, if they were unwilling to, to resign their seats and put their revised opinions to the test of by-elections.[18] (Few members took up the challenge. Two who did, one of them Lord Ashley, lost their seats. Ashley found many 'gentlemen' for him, but not enough of them to overcome the protectionism of the farmers.[19] Lord Lincoln, standing for re-election at Nottinghamshire South as a consequence of taking a place in the cabinet, was defeated by a protectionist candidate who was sent an agent and £2,000 by the Central Protection Society.[20])

Constituency pressure from the tenant farmers was a major reason for the unexpectedly large size of the Conservative opposition to repeal in the House of Commons in 1846. The other was the emergence of the previously silent squire, Lord George Bentinck, as a forceful and tireless leader of the dissidents[21] and the flowering into outright opposition of Disraeli, who in a series of bruising, sarcastic speeches voiced for others too timid or too well-bred to speak in such accents themselves the rage and frustration which they felt at Peel's 'apostasy'. Disraeli's theme was the constitutional one that Peel was destroying the meaning of party and therefore the basis of parliamentary government. Whatever members' opinions about free trade might be, he argued, they could all agree to 'oppose the introduction of free politics'.

> Above all, maintain the line of demarcation between parties; for it is only by maintaining the independence of party that you can maintain the integrity of public men, and the power and influence of Parliament itself.[22]

Had they accepted the case for free trade, the agriculturalists might not have given a scruple for the constitutional argument; being against free trade, they found it to their liking.

The 241 Conservatives who voted against repeal on its third reading in May were unable to save the corn laws; almost the whole of the Whig opposition sided with the government, giving repeal a majority of nearly 100. An attempt to reach an all-party compromise in the Lords on the basis of a small, fixed duty of about 5s per quarter came to nothing. But in June the protectionists took their revenge on Peel when 74 of them, thinking it more important to overthrow a government which had 'betrayed' them than to follow their habitual instincts on matters relating to Ireland, joined with the Whigs to defeat the government's bill to renew coercion in Ireland. Peel at once resigned, explaining to his cabinet colleagues in words of delicious, but probably unintentional, irony that 'a Conservative government should be supported by a Conservative party'.[23]

Historians have long since ceased to interpret the repeal of the corn laws as a great class victory signifying the triumph of the urban bourgeoisie over the landed aristocracy. For another generation and more the membership of the House of Commons and of cabinets continued to reflect the staying power of the landed class. Indeed, it is possible to view repeal in the same light as the 1832 reform act, as a timely concession which enabled the ruling class to assuage middle-class resentments, detach the middle classes from their inferiors and thus retard the march of democracy. To see matters in that light is, of course, to look through Peel's spectacles. Repeal may have been timely, but as the protectionists who went down to defeat in 1846 stand witness, it was not a concession. Squire and farmer lived, at any rate, to see their worst fears confounded: English farming entered upon its mid-Victorian golden age, enjoying a prosperity which lasted until the great depression of the late 1870s and the flooding into the country of American grain.

There remains the question whether the split in parliament over the repeal of the corn laws between a largely pro-repeal Whig opposition and a largely anti-repeal Conservative rank and file reflects to any significant degree a difference in the class basis of the two parties. Throughout the mid-19th century the Conservatives were a more predominantly landed party than their opponents: between 1833 and 1868 more than 50 per cent of new Conservative MPs were substantial landowners, against only 28 per cent of Whigs and Liberals. And in the same period the ratio of landed gentlemen to businessmen among the new MPs in the Liberal parliamentary party changed from 6:2 to 6:5, whereas the ratio among Conservatives changed from 8:1 to only 9:2.[24] Even so, the Liberal Party, thanks to its Whig element, was still the more aristocratic of the two parties as late as 1868, as Anthony Trollope wrote in his novel, *Phineas Redux*.

> There is probably more of the flavour of political aristocracy to be found still remaining among our liberal leading statesmen than among their opponents. A conservative Cabinet is, doubtless, never deficient in dukes and lords, and the sons of such; but conservative dukes and lords are recruited here and there, and as recruits, are new to the business, whereas among the old Whigs a halo of statecraft has, for ages past, so strongly pervaded and enveloped certain great families, that the power in the world of politics thus produced still remains, and is even yet efficacious in creating a feeling of exclusiveness. . . . The old hereditary Whig Cabinet ministers must, no doubt, by this time have learned to feel themselves at home with strange neighbours at their elbows. But still with them something of the feeling of high blood, of rank, and of living in a park with deer about it, remains. They still entertain a pride in their Cabinets, and have, at any rate, not as yet submitted themselves to a conjuror. The Charles James Fox element of liberality still holds its own, and the fragrance of Cavendish is essential.[25]

No doubt Trollope overdrew the picture; but an attempt to describe the House of Commons in 1846 as divided between a pro-repeal party of Whig businessmen and an anti-repeal party of Conservative landowners will not succeed. Even within the Conservative Party the landed and non-landed sections split against repeal in approximately the same ratio of 2:1.[26] What is significant, however, is that those Conservative members of parliament who *represented* landed constituencies voted against repeal far more solidly than those who did not. The breakdown shows that 86 per cent of the Conservatives who sat for the counties and the universities voted against repeal, 63 per cent of those who sat for boroughs with an electorate smaller than 500, and only 50 per cent of those who represented the larger boroughs. It was the farmers who stiffened the resolve of the protectionist Conservatives, just as it was the town-dwellers who gave sustenance to the liberalism of the Whigs.

Protectionist anger at Peel for abandoning the corn laws was heightened by the language he used in announcing his government's resignation in the House of Commons on 29 June, in a speech described by one protectionist journalist as 'no doubt the sorest and probably the most incautious' that he ever made.[27] Peel, to everyone's astonishment, eulogised Richard Cobden, whose speeches had so inflamed that landed class which the Conservative prime minister had said repeatedly in 1846 it was his purpose to uphold and defend, as the man to whom the credit for the triumph of free trade was due. Nor did he stop there. Direct insult he saved for the peroration.

> In relinquishing power I shall leave a name severely censured I fear by many who on public grounds deeply regret the severance of party ties, deeply regret that severance, not from interested or personal motives, but from the firm conviction that fidelity to party engagements – the existence and maintenance of a great party – constitutes a powerful instrument of government. I shall surrender power severely censured also by others, who from no interested motives, adhere to the principle of protection, considering the maintenance of it to be essential to the welfare and interests of the country; I shall leave a name execrated by every monopolist who, from less honourable motives, clamours for protection because it conduces to his own individual benefit; but it may be that I shall leave a name sometimes remembered with expressions of good will in the abodes of those whose lot it is to labour, and to earn their daily bread by the sweat of their brow, when they shall recruit their exhausted strength with abundant and untaxed food, the sweeter because it is no longer leavened by a sense of injustice.[28]

The question whether, if the corn laws really had leavened the bread of the poor with a sense of injustice, some apology was due to them from one of the chief leaveners, does not seem to have clouded Peel's mind. And though he was careful to distinguish between patriotic protectionists and 'monopolists', using the latter word at all – a favourite of the Anti-Corn Law League – was a signal that he meant never again to lead the Conservative Party.

For the future of party politics in Great Britain the most important consequence of the repeal of the corn laws was that the split in the Conservative ranks was destined to remain permanent. The protectionist wing, slightly enlarged in the years immediately after 1846 by the return of some Peelites to the fold, carried the mantle of Conservatism into the future. Defeats at the 1847 elections cut into the Peelites' strength and left them a force in the House of Commons of little more than 40 members. Peelites and Protectionists operated as separate parties, each with its own whips and election managers, though the Protectionists, benefiting from the virtual identification in most constituencies of the local Conservative association and the local protection society, were the more solidly organised. At Westminster the Peelites, even before Peel's death in 1850, had no acknowledged leader. Strength of numbers allowed the Protectionists to behave as the authentic bearers of the Conservative tradition. The Peelites, eager to protect the free-trade settlement, lent their support to Lord John Russell's Whig government; the Protectionists functioned as the regular opposition under Lord Stanley, who, impressed by the size of Conservative resistance to Peel in the 1846 debates, had abandoned his intention to give a silent vote in favour of repeal and had spoken and voted against it. He also overcame his initial refusal to imagine a Conservative government which rested on anything other than Peelite principles and Peelite men; and by the summer of 1846 he had tacitly accepted the leadership of the Protectionist Party.

There were thus three parties in the field, the Whig/Liberals, the Peelites and the Protectionists.[29] Conservative division handed office to the Whigs and Liberals for a generation. Not until 1874 did the Conservative Party again win a majority at the polls. The Conservatives suffered from the distribution of seats in the electoral system, which gave the population in the towns a disproportionate share of the representation in the House of Commons; but their great handicap was their attachment to a narrow agrarian interest. The great landowning aristocracy, many of whose members were more richly rewarded by the income from urban properties, coal mines or railways on their land or the dividends from capital investments than they were by agricultural rents, had displayed some willingness to compromise in 1846. The squirearchy and the tenant farmers, less fortunately placed, had not. They were the backbone of the party, able to maintain it as the largest single party in the state, but numerically too weak even so and economically too obviously tied to a declining sectional interest – by 1846 farming occupied only 25 per cent of the population and provided an even smaller share of the national income – to elevate it above the status of what Eric Hobsbawm has called 'a minority pressure group stiffened by a bloc of fox-hunting back-bench MPs'.[30]

Between 1846 and 1852 various attempts were tried to re-unite the Conservative Party, the most critical of which took place in 1851, when Russell's government, beaten in the House of Commons on a Radical motion to equalise the suffrage qualification in the counties and boroughs, resigned. The queen sent for Stanley, who sought to bring the leading Peelites, including William Gladstone, into a Conservative government. The negotiations failed from the start. Personalities played their part. Gladstone especially, but the other Peelites as well, found the prospect of serving either with or under Disraeli, Peel's fiercest assailant in 1845 and 1846, and now the Protectionist leader in the Commons, distasteful. Protection, too, continued to stand in the way. The regular Conservatives under Stanley had not yet made their peace with free trade. Having branded Peel a traitor, they could not themselves slough off the corn laws in a day. And a severe drop in wheat prices in the years from 1849 to 1851, which seemed to confirm the farmers' fears of the consequences of repeal, was the background to a national campaign to restore the corn laws conducted by the National Association for the Protection of British Industry and Capital. That campaign helped the Protectionists to win several by-elections and convinced them that it would be foolish to risk alienating the support of their bedrock supporters in the shires by abandoning the food issue before trying it at one more general election. In his negotiations with the Peelites, Stanley could not avoid making a small fixed duty on imported corn a necessary part of the programme of his prospective administration. Office on the terms that Stanley proposed was unacceptable to the Peelites. Stanley declined to form a minority government and Russell and the Whigs came back to office.

Never sure of the support of the Radicals or the Irish and dependent on Peelite votes for their majority, the Whigs remained precariously in office for another year, until defeat on a bill to reorganise the militia drove them once more to resign. In February 1852 Lord Derby (Stanley had inherited his father's earldom nine months earlier) formed a minority Protectionist administration. Its legislative record was necessarily undistinguished. But the elections which were fought in the summer of 1852, and which failed to give the Protectionists a majority, had two important consequences. The first was that the debate over free trade *versus* protection – a debate which had been at or near the forefront of party politics since the passing of the 1815 corn law – was at last buried, not to be resurrected until the first years of the 20th century. The second was that the Protectionists' behaviour at the elections – the excessive use of bribery and the unashamed appeal to the anti-Catholic sentiments which had been so prominent during the Maynooth debates and which had been fanned into a flame by the so-called 'papal aggression' of 1850–51* – ended whatever chance remained that the two wings of the Conservative Party might settle their differences. All the opposition sections of the House of Commons joined together to defeat the Protectionist government on Disraeli's budget in December – the last, tumultuous night of the week-long budget debate was the occasion of Disraeli's undeservedly famous and not very accurate taunt that 'England does not love coalitions' – and the incipient liberalism of the Peelites brought them at last to make a formal compact with the Whigs. The coalition government which Lord Aberdeen, who had been the foreign secretary in Peel's cabinet, formed at the end of 1852 included all the prominent Whigs and Peelites. In that union the great Victorian Liberal Party was conceived, though it was to remain in embryo until the pact made at the Willis' Tea Rooms in 1859 brought it into the light of day. And

---

* In September, 1850 a papal brief proclaimed the restoration of the Roman Catholic hierarchy in England (extinct since the mid-16th century) and Cardinal Wiseman was given the title, archbishop of Westminster. Protestant England was incensed by the alleged purpose of the Vatican to 'govern' Roman Catholic sees in England. The pope was burned in effigy throughout the land and the more rabid sections of the Protectionist Party looked forward to reaping an electoral harvest from the pope's 'aggression'. Temperatures were lowered when Russell's government introduced a bill to forbid the assumption of 'territorial' ecclesiastical titles by the Roman Catholic episcopacy. The Ecclesiastical Titles Bill passed by very large majorities, opposed only by the Peelites, Irish Roman Catholic MPs and a handful of Radicals, in 1851. The act was never enforced.

by that union the Conservative Party was condemned to the wilderness for a generation, secure, to use the language of a later age, in its heartland, but without the power (and, perhaps, without the imagination) to break new electoral ground.

7

REFORM AND THE DISPOSSESSED

The framers of the 1832 reform act, by introducing a uniform £10-householder franchise and removing ancient franchises such as the scot-and-lot (for a man who paid the local rate called a 'scot') and the potwalloper (for a man with his own hearth, who cooked his own meals), sought to alter the balance of the electorate in the towns decisively in favour of the middle classes. The act fulfilled their intentions. The working-class element of the population had never formed an important part of the electorate except in those places where the town corporations had been liberal in the creation of freemen; after 1832 its position was even weaker than before. At a time when the average house rental (though prices varied throughout the country) was somewhere between £4 and £8 a year, there were very few manual labourers who qualified for the vote as £10 householders. The old freeman vote, moreover, by which town corporations had brought a number of working men on to the registers, was retained after 1832 only for the lifetime of existing freemen and their eldest sons. Those freemen who did retain the vote were concentrated in the old, smaller boroughs where they were virtually in fee to their political masters and peculiarly susceptible to bribery. The new industrial proletariat of the north and midlands, and also of London, was frozen out of parliamentary politics. And since there was little inflationary effect to bring working-class householders up to the £10 mark, there they remained. The parliamentary return (or papers) of the number of working-class voters in 1865–66, on the eve of the second reform act, showed that only one-quarter of the voters in the English boroughs could be described as working-class. In the north the proportion was much lower: in Leeds, for example, it was only 7 per cent.[1] The urban electorate of early and mid-Victorian England was socially exclusive. It was also pre-industrial in character, made up chiefly of shopkeepers, artisans and members of the professions. Representatives of the new capital being raised by manufactures, the industrial magnates, were conspicuously few in the House of Commons. Even the old argument that the country was divided into self-contained 'interests' and that the lower, unfranchised elements of an 'interest' were 'virtually represented' in parliament by their superiors could not easily be sustained in reference to the factory hands.

Two consequences flowed from those facts. The first was that there was little reason for the established political parties to adopt policies or frame legislation with a view to ingratiating themselves with the working-class majority of the nation. A small number of Conservative members of parliament in the latter 1830s championed the cause of the factory operatives and even, to some degree, of the Chartists; and in one or two constituencies there was an overt alliance between the Tory candidates and local Chartists. But the spasm which went by the name of Tory Radicalism was controlled by the reality of working-class electoral impotence. (The scores of Conservative Operative Societies which were established in the 1830s were intended to bind workers to Church-and-King Toryism, not to initiate Conservatives into the mysteries of the workers' grievances and aspirations.[2]) The second consequence, entirely obvious, was that the electoral system left no scope for the direct participation by the working classes in parliamentary politics. They had therefore to seek extra-parliamentary means of persuading, by argument or by threat of disorder, the political parties to take notice of them.

It was not only the urban workers, of course, who were dispossessed. The most overt expressions of social anger in the previous half-century had come from the poor in the countryside. Food riots and outbreaks of machine-breaking were essentially rural forms of protest. The alleged 'deference' of the lower orders in the landed hierarchy was undoubtedly as much sullen resignation as well-tempered obedience. The great agricultural estates, which Cobbett called 'factories for making corn and wheat', were worked by ill-paid labourers whose customary rights – to wood and peat for fuel, for instance, and to land for their own cultivation and grazing – had been largely taken away from them. The agricultural labourers formed, not a genuine peasantry with its plots of land, but a landless, rural proletariat, with no expectation that they or their offspring would rise to the status of tenantry. They were socially immobile, whose only hope was to remain farm labourers for so long as the agrarian sector of the economy, steadily declining as a proportion of the national economy, offered them subsistence employment. They lived, on many estates, 'in rows of cottages . . . away from any village . . . in the shadow of the great farmhouse, so that their lives could be as clipped and disciplined as the hedges'.[3]

It was nevertheless from the towns, London and the northern towns especially, that the working-class challenge to the existing order came in the 1830s and 1840s. In those decades, most cruelly in the years between 1838 and 1842 – the last of which was the most depressed year of the century, giving rise to the phrase, 'the hungry forties' – the economy of Great Britain passed through a crisis of early modern industrial capitalism. The most obvious evidence of the crisis, as Eric Hobsbawm has written, was 'the high wind of social discontent' which blew across the country. At no other period since the 17th century had the common people been 'so persistently, profoundly, and often desperately dissatisfied'.[4]

Nor at any other period, perhaps, had so many of them been so well informed. The age was athirst for information, as organisations like the Mechanics' Institutes and the Society for the Diffusion of Useful Knowledge, begun in the 1820s, testified; and if those institutions were derided by the Radicals as organs of Whig propaganda (they tended, at any rate, against the founders' intentions, to attract a middle-class clientele), the Radicals themselves, in a host of penny publications and cheap tracts like Cobbett's wonderfully successful and influential *Politi-*

cal Register, had been contributing to the 'march of mind' and the political education of the masses. 'Knowledge, education are opening the eyes of the humblest', Thomas Carlyle wrote in *Signs of the Times*, published in 1829; 'are increasing the number of thinking minds without limit.'[5] The state hung back from providing national primary education (and did so until 1870), but literacy rates were improving, thanks to the efforts of the various denominational and voluntary schools. Gin palaces declined as sober coffee houses and teashops proliferated; by the 1840s there were nearly 2,000 such meeting places, many of them plentifully stocked with newspapers, magazines and quarterly reviews and serving as reading rooms and discussion centres.[6] (Working-class temperance was especially strong in Scotland, where it helped both to draw men into Chartism – the Scottish Chartist leader, Robert Cranston, ran a famous temperance tea room – and to dilute the movement of revolutionary force.[7]) Not that self-improvement was exclusively linked to teetotalism: by 1849 there were more than 5,000 public houses and nearly 3,000 beershops in England which served as reading rooms for working men.[8]

In the background to the great Chartist surge of the late 1830s and early 1840s lay a succession of disappointments and setbacks for the working class. The Radical group within parliament failed, after 1832, to make a significant impact on legislation, divided as it was within itself, virtually leaderless and, after the 1837 elections, diminished in numbers. The most important section of the Radicals, the Philosophic Radicals whose intellectual leadership came from John Stuart Mill, were, at any rate, not much interested in industrial questions such as the ten-hour day for factory workers, although they were believers in universal manhood suffrage. In the early 1830s a number of attempts were made to organise the workers in large trade unions (the ban on workers' combinations had been lifted in 1825), the most important and grandiose of which was the Grand National Consolidated Trades Union, formed by the cooperative socialist, Robert Owen. The GNCTU established a formidable federal structure to link trade unionists across the country, from local branches to grand lodges, in one working-class movement. But from the outset it faced what quickly were proved to be insurmountable difficulties. Its root-and-branch socialism and its utopian call for a complete reorganisation of society on cooperative principles to win 'for the productive classes a complete dominion over the fruits of their own industry'[9] were too advanced to attract the sympathy of most workers. The four major trade unions in the country, representing the builders, the spinners, the potters and the clothiers, stayed outside the GNCTU, and when the financial burden of supporting the Derbyshire trade unionists who were locked out of work by their employers and of supporting striking workers in London and the west country used up all its funds, the organisation collapsed. It had lasted only six months. The lesson of its failure, that direct political action was the only way forward, was reinforced by the treatment meted out to the leaders of the Dorsetshire union, the Friendly Society of Agricultural Labourers, based at Tolpuddle. The object of the society was the simple and legal one of gaining fair wages for its members; yet six of its leaders were arrested, convicted on a flimsy charge of administering illegal secret oaths to its members, and given the severe sentence of transportation for seven years to Australia.

The weakness of trade unionism and the absence of a powerful working-class voice in the House of Commons led working-class leaders to the conclusion that little could be achieved until the fight for universal manhood suffrage was won. Chartism was born of that despair and that conviction. Indeed, the link between the founding of the Chartist movement in 1838 and the failed trade union movement of a few years earlier was provided by the Dorchester Committee which was established by William Lovett, a London joiner who had been a student at the London Mechanics' Institute, in 1834 to organise protest meetings (25,000 marched in London) and gather petitions against the transportation of the 'Tolpuddle martyrs'. It was Lovett who, with the editor of the *Poor Man's Guardian*, Henry Hetherington, founded the London Working Men's Association in 1836 and it was that organisation which gave birth to the National Charter of 1838. Chartism was a petitioning movement which took its place in the long tradition of such movements in English history.

Its stated aims, the famous six points of the Charter, were all constitutional: manhood suffrage, equal electoral districts, annual parliaments, payment of members of parliament, no property qualifications for members and a secret ballot. But Chartism drew its strength, not from abstract notions of the rights of men, but from the daily hardships endured by the people, even if the aspirations which it embraced and the arguments which it spawned were too complex to make it what Joseph Stephens, the Tory leader of the ten-hours and anti-poor law campaigns, called it, simply 'a knife and fork question'.

The deep economic crisis which Great Britain passed through between 1837 and 1842, a recession signalled by the failed harvest of 1836, sent bread prices soaring after a record low price for wheat of 36s a quarter at the end of 1835. Two years later a financial crisis, which brought a halt to the industrial boom of the early 1830s, led to mounting unemployment, especially in Lancashire and the midlands. Cyclical trade depression and the black years of the early 1840s coincided with the peak of the Chartist movement. But the underlying malaise was the failure of the working class throughout the decades of the early industrial revolution to gain a proportionate share of the accumulating wealth of the country. In 1849, when Chartist energies were spent and England was entering a period of social stability, the returns of the poor law commissioners revealed that nearly one million paupers were receiving relief either in or out of the workhouse. And that figure masks the true extent of poverty and destitution, since the poor laws were only one form of relief in an age which distributed alms through a wide range of private charitable agencies. Whether the historians' debate about the rise or fall in the workers' standard of living between 1815 and 1850 will ever be resolved,[10] it is evident that, even if it were rising, it was doing so more slowly than it was for the middle classes, so that the gap in incomes between the two classes was widening.

The redistribution of income and wealth was not yet a question openly discussed in party politics. Cobden and his Financial Reform Association, formed in 1848, brought it near the light of day by pressing for a general preference for direct over indirect taxation and by 1860 Lord Robert Cecil, the future Marquess of Salisbury and Conservative prime minister, was warning his party that the incidence of taxation had become the vital field upon which the contending classes in society would do battle, 'a struggle between those who have, to keep what they have got, and those who have not, to get it'.[11] But at mid-century that issue, which was eventually to dominate, as it does still dominate, democratic politics, had yet to make its urgency felt inside the House of Commons. In 1851 England congratulated itself on its wealth and manufacturing progress at the Great Exhibition housed in the Crystal Palace. William Johnston, a Tory barrister and journalist, viewed the spectacle with misgivings.

> As regards the great mass of the people, there is no reason for congratulation upon the progress of wealth, virtue, or happiness. The mercantile middle class has become opulent through the use of cheap substitutes for labour, but the labourers sink in the scale of social existence. ... In the acquisition of wealth the nation has made great progress, but in that distribution of it which seems best calculated to impart moderate comfort on the one hand, and to abate the pomp of superior position and insolence of riches on the other, the science of modern times is at fault, while the selfishness connected with it revels for the present in unabated triumph.[12]

Curiously, one of the most hated pieces of 19th-century legislation, and one which has retained the reputation for being an instrument of oppression in the class war, the new poor law of 1834, stemmed not only from the Whigs' determination to contain riot and disorder, but also from their intention (whether misdirected is a separate question) to improve the lot of the poor. Two phenomena of the early 19th century, the rising burden of the poor rate (which climbed from £500,000 in 1750 to nearly £8,000,000 in the peak year of 1817) and the regular incidence of rural crime and lawlessness in the agrarian south (culminating in the Captain Swing riots of 1830), persuaded the Whigs that the long-mooted question of the reform of the system of poor relief could no longer with safety be left unanswered. For decades the prevailing system of leaving it to local magistrates to supplement low wages with relief payments (based on the price of bread) – in other words, establishing a rough-and-ready minimum wage and paying it out of local rates – had been held to be the root cause of rural pauperism. The allowance system, as it was called, was believed to have three unwanted consequences: it blurred the distinction between the pauper who received poor relief and the independent labourer who did not by equalising their wages; it therefore encouraged employers to hire relief-assisted labour and so depressed the general level of wages; and it encouraged couples to produce children, thus adding to the 'surplus population' (which Thomas Robert Malthus had argued was the root of the trouble) and aggravating the evil. In short a vicious circle was operating: surplus population led to unemployment; unemployment led to the payment of allowances; the payment of allowances led to population growth. The system was pauperising the rural population and producing riot; the solution was to reform the system.

Contemporaries' view of the contribution of the allowance system to rising poor rates was probably exaggerated; the system was, at any rate, being abandoned after 1815 and the cost of poor relief seems also to have been declining.[13] The Whigs, however, accepted the truth of the charges against the system and in 1832 they appointed a royal commission to inquire into its operation. The commission's report recommended a thorough recasting of the system. The chief recommendations were these. First, relief was to be given to 'able-bodied' paupers only in conditions (preferably inside a workhouse, though the bill introduced in 1834 did not *require* a local authority to build one) that would make relief a 'less eligible' choice for the working man than employment. In other words, the so-called surplus population which was out of work was supposed to be idle and feckless, not unable to find employment. Second, the old parish structure of relief was to be replaced by a new administrative arrangement. Large poor law unions were to be established, with local elections to fill the boards of guardians, and central commissioners were to see that the new provisions were enforced. Control of poor relief, that is, was to be taken away from the squires who served as local magistrates and who were judged 'guilty' of distributing the 'demoralising' allowances.

The report furnished the essential provisions of the Whig bill of 1834, which passed into law with little opposition (at most the scattered votes of about 50 Radical, Irish and Tory MPs), chiefly because landowners on both sides of the House of Commons were grateful for any measure which might save them money on the poor rate and which might help to produce social peace in the countryside. Yet the new law was a dramatic challenge to the notions of a deferential, hierarchical society in which men of all ranks were bound together by ties of loyalty and mutual regard for each others' well-being. By freeing labour from the degrading and pauperising allowance system and exposing it to the revivifying influence of the free market, the new system would release productive energies, create a larger wages fund and so demonstrate that the surplus population was an artificial one which a progressive, expanding economy would absorb. The 1834 act thus marked a startling reversal. Malthusian theory, enunciated in the *Essay on the Principles of Population* published in 1798, held that there was a fixed 'wages fund', a fixed proportion of the national wealth, and that as the national wealth increased by an arithmetic progression so did population increase by a far more rapid geometric progression, thus wiping out the economic gains and leaving the 'surplus population' poorer than before. That theory had seeped into the official mind. In 1834 it seeped, almost unnoticed, away.

The new poor law was testimony to the Whigs' belief in the freedom of contract between labour and capital. In 1833 Lord Grey told Henry Brougham, who was one of the strongest advocates of the new law in the cabinet, that trade unions which existed to advance, or prevent a reduction of, wages were a social evil, since they exercised a permanent limitation on that freedom. 'No persons are more grievously oppressed by them than many classes of the workmen themselves.'[14] The same faith in the free operation of the labour market, the same confidence in its benefits to the workers themselves, underlay the new poor law.[15] But the view supposed that the individuals who composed society were free agents able to discover their self-interest and conduct their lives accordingly, the very individuals, that is, who were incompatible with a deferential society. As much as the great reform act and the repeal of the corn laws, the new poor law constituted a direct assault on the old aristocratic order.

The new poor law, framed to meet the sporadic violence and peculiar economic conditions of the agrarian south, was introduced into the midlands early in 1836 and extended to the north at the end of the year. For two years a fierce agitation, led by men who had made their mark in the campaign begun at the beginning of the decade for factory reform, was waged against the act in the north. The agitation brought together Tories (many of them Evangelical in their religious leanings) and Radicals united in their opposition to the *laisser-faire*, liberal ethos of the day, which stood in the way of legislative interference in industrial relations.[16] Much of the opposition was rooted in the misapprehension (excited in people's minds by factory reformers who were happy to add any grist to their mill) that poor relief itself was to be abandoned. Much came also from anger at the government's intention to make entry into a workhouse the degrading condition of receiving relief, as if poverty were a sin. The act had been framed to meet the circumstances arising from low wages and seasonal unemployment in the agricultural counties. Conditions in the north were different: a chronic shortage of labour and good wages during manufacturing prosperity, mass unemployment (especially in the building and weaving trades) during recession. The northern protest against the poor law was part of the fight for shorter hours and higher wages for factory operatives. The law was depicted as a device to frighten men by the prospect of the workhouse into accepting any terms of employment; and new regulations more restrictive of a parish's ability to provide relief for persons born outside its boundaries gave rise to fears that child labour would be imported from the south to work in the mills.

Since the allowance system had rarely been practised in the north and poor rates there were much lower than in the south, middle-class ratepayers joined the opposition to the act, which would entail considerable expense in reorganising the administration of poor relief without bringing the benefits intended for the agricultural districts. The Tory-Radical alliance already forged over the factory issue proved, however, impossible to sustain. For one thing, the poor law commissioners in the north were extremely cautious in implementing the act. In many places they allowed money relief in aid of wages and relief by assisted payment of rent to continue. Moreover, it was difficult for Radicals and Tories, so used to opposing one another, to cooperate either in boycotting elections to the boards of guardians or in electing a common slate of candidates. By the middle of 1838 the mass-petitioning campaign against the poor law was on the wane. A bill introduced in the House of Commons by the Tory, John Fielden, to repeal the act attracted only 19 votes: many local Tories in the north opposed the act, but the parliamentary party did not. The *Northern Star*, which was to become the leading organ of Feargus O'Connor's militant wing of the Chartist movement and which had been founded in 1837 to voice protests against the poor law and employment conditions in the textile trade, came to the conclusion that popular agitation was impotent to compel parliament and that only a radical reform of parliament itself could bring about the changes sought by the workers. The anti-poor law movement and the ten-hours campaign never quite lost their separate identities; but they became merged in the greater campaign for the Charter.

Chartism was, of course, much more than an enlargement of the anti-poor law and ten-hours campaigns, just as it was much more than what, many years ago, Elie Halévy called it, 'the blind revolt of hunger'.[17] The demand for universal suffrage and annual parliaments, the most urgently pressed of the six points of the Charter, had its origin in a long-standing radical tradition. Economic distress swelled the Chartist tide; it does not on its own account for the existence of the movement. The stark despair of 1842 produced the Miners' Association of Great Britain and Ireland, which gained 70,000 members within two years, but the union forswore violence, narrowed its sights to gaining better conditions and higher wages for its members, and eschewed Chartism. Chartism fed on conviction, not simply anger. The rich diversity of Chartism's membership (free-traders as well as fierce opponents of the Manchester school, trade unionists and Owenite cooperativists) and the conflicting aspirations of its leaders (those who sought an alliance with the middle classes against the landed oligarchy and those who wished to build a purely working-class movement), as well as the quarrel over methods (the moral force of persuasion by peaceful petitioning or the physical force of threatening to use, or in extremity actually resorting to, arms) make Chartism incapable of swift definition.[18]

The diffusion of its aims and the multiplicity of its grievances may have weakened Chartism as a practical political movement, though they enriched it as an expression of the maturing of working-class pride and confidence. By comparison with Chartism, the Anti-Corn Law League no doubt gained from having a single, identifiable enemy and a single objective. But the heart of the matter was that the League spoke the economic orthodoxy of the day, that it had powerful friends in the House of Commons and that many of its supporters in the constituencies had the ultimate weapon of the vote. When Lord Grey warned parliament in 1834 against being moved 'by a constant and active pressure from without to the adoption of any measures the strict necessity of which has not been fully proved, and which are not strictly regulated by a careful attention to the settled institutions of the country',[19] he was not speaking hypocrisy, but he was very near to speaking cant. When the objective of 'pressure from without', such as the repeal of the test and corporation acts or Catholic emancipation or the abolition of slavery, coincided with his opinions, he did not solemnly pronounce against extra-parliamentary agitation. In 1831–32 he had been happy to exploit it. Chartism's fatal weakness was that it had neither parliamentary strength nor the means of gaining it. It had to develop into a revolutionary movement or collapse.

Many reasons may be adduced to explain why a 'revolutionary consciousness' did not seize workers' minds in the first half of the 19th century: the desperate, violence-inclined representatives of the old, declining crafts like handloom-weaving were set apart from the transport workers, miners and cotton operatives of the new economy, who were groping for ways to make the most out of industrial progress, not to overturn the social order; the primitive national communications network made planned uprising a perilously difficult business; the decentralisation of the country's legal and administrative institutions made a *coup d'état* at the centre a strategy of doubtful issue; and revolution by general strike required a far more comprehensive development of trade unionism. There is, in addition, undoubted force to the argument that no revolution succeeds unless the ruling class is so divided within itself or so demoralised by panic that it is incapable of suppressing rebellion. The old 'Whig' argument that England was saved its 'year of revolution' in 1848 by the wisdom of an entrenched ruling class, confident enough to absorb a new electorate in 1832 and gratify it in 1846 and supple enough to assuage working-class frustrations by measures of social reform, is not a foolish one.

The economic changes which came over Great Britian in the first half of the 19th century should not be exaggerated. In 1850 there were still ten times as many agricultural workers as cotton factory hands. And the revolution in transport, marked in its early phase by canal-building and in the 1830s and 1840s by the coming of the railways and the 'parliamentary train', crucial though it was for the release of industrial energies, did not at once overcome the barriers of distance which left the Durham miner knowing almost nothing of the existence of the London docker. Poor communications retarded the growth of working-class solidarity. Yet improved transport and the relentless concentration of population in towns and cities were breaking down regional isolation. England was becoming less a collection of separate regions, each with its own centres – at Exeter and Bristol or at Norwich and King's Lynn – and more a geographical and economic unity. And one of the consequences was that in place of the ancient wisdom that local needs were the responsibility of local leaders and local institutions the argument that there were national problems which required national solutions was gaining ground. The 1830s witnessed an explosion of information. Rural poverty was more easily hidden than the squalor of the disease-ridden, death-inducing large towns. Royal commissions replaced select committees and members of parliament discovered that to rise in politics required the drudgery of reading the blue books. Flowing from royal commissions on the poor law, on child labour in the mines, on health conditions, in 1844 on the very general subject of 'large towns and populous districts', facts invaded the early Victorian mind. And that mind had been prepared by Jeremy Bentham and his followers and by the Evangelical Christian moralists to look with horror and compassion on the lives of Burke's 'swinish multitude' and to seek ways to mitigate the horror and make the compassion effective.

Bentham's dictum that the end of legislation was 'the greatest happiness of the greatest number' (the phrase came originally from the Irish philosopher, Francis Hutcheson) had implications radically different from Locke's statement that the end of government was the preservation of property. Bentham's starting-point led logically to the conclusion that governments must intervene in social and industrial relations to regulate them for the greatest welfare of all the people. That notion underlay the 'revolution in government' of the 1830s and 1840s: the 1834 poor law, the 1842 mines act (which forbade the employment for work underground of women and boys under the age of ten), the 1847 ten hours act and the 1848 health of towns act (which empowered a central board of health to compel localities to supply adequate water to their inhabitants) were all backed by central inspectorates whose duty it was to see that the acts were enforced. The offical mind was deeply impregnated with Benthamism. Royal commissions were in theory composed of impartial men seeking facts; in reality, because it was necessary to appoint to them men with an interest in and understanding of the subjects, they were dominated by Benthamites like Nassau Senior and Edwin Chadwick, who came to the facts with a solution already in their minds. The combination of Benthamite radicalism and Christian conscience, the latter pricked into activity by the missionary work accomplished during two generations by Evangelicals like William Wilberforce,[20] was powerful. It met stern resistance from the *laisser-faire* political economists and their disciples, who denied the utility of government interference in the contractual arrangements of the market, and from traditionalists, who resented the undermining by central institutions and central regulatory boards of the ancient governing of the people by justice of the peace and parish vestry. But the combination was powerful enough to persuade parliament to place on the statute books acts of social reform which laid the foundations of the welfare state.[21]

One way of stating the matter is to say that in those years 'it came to be felt that the community as a whole had a responsibility for the minimum welfare of the individuals who composed it'.[22] A visitor to England, Theodore Fontane, remarked that the poor were not about to revolt because although 'the state does nothing *for* the people, neither does it do anything *against* them'.[23] For whatever reasons what happened in the 1830s and 1840s was that 'the popular movements never became revolutionary and the revolutionary movements never became popular'.[24] There is no need to find reasons, or provide apologies, for the *failure* of the working class to develop a revolutionary consciousness. It may be that the long work of British historical experience had (and has) been to imbue its citizens with an understanding, or 'consciousness', of the blessings of life lived under the rule of law. An historian of popular disturbances in early industrial England has written that for revolutionary upheaval to take place 'there needs to be a group equipped with the kind of ideology to make them want to seize power when the opportunity arises'.[25] In constitutional regimes subject to law a different ideology may prevail, one that leads us to speak of the *success* of the working class in developing an unrevolutionary consciousness. In 1848, the year of revolution throughout continental Europe, Anthony Trollope wrote from Ireland, where he was employed by the post office, to his mother in Tuscany.

> I get letters from England, asking me whether I am not afraid to have my wife and children in this country, whereas all I hear or see of Irish rows is in the columns of the *Times* newspaper. . . . Here in Ireland the meaning of the word Communism – or even social revolution – is not understood. The people have not the remotest notion of attempting to improve their worldy condition by making the difference between the employer and the employed less marked. Revolution here means a row. Some like a row, having little or nothing to lose. These are revolutionists and call for pikes. Others are anti-revolutionists, having something to lose and dreading a row. These condemn the pikes, and demand more soldiers and police.

There is no notion of anything beyond this; – no conception of any theory such as that of Louis Blanc [the French socialist]. My own idea is that there is no ground to fear any general rising either in England or Ireland. I think there is too much intelligence in England for any large body of men to look for any sudden improvement; and not enough intelligence in Ireland for any body of men at all to conceive the possibility of social improvement.[26]

REFERENCES

1. THE OLD ORDER

1. P. D. G. Thomas, 'Sir Roger Newdigate's Essays on Party, *c.*1760', *English Historical Review*, April 1987, pp. 395–96.
2. See A. F. Foord, 'The Waning of the Influence of the Crown', *English Historical Review*, July, 1921, and R. Pares, *King George III and the Politicians* (Oxford, 1953), Chapter 6.
3. The most forthright argument for the importance of party before 1830 is to be found in F. O'Gorman, *The Emergence of the British Two-Party System, 1760–1832* (London, 1982). See also B. W. Hill, *British Parliamentary Parties, 1742–1832* (London, 1985), and the same author's 'Executive Monarchy and the Challenge of Parties, 1689–1832: Two Concepts of Government and Two Historiographical Interpretations', *Historical Journal*, September 1970.
4. Anon., *Observations on Two Pamphlets (Lately Published) Attributed to Mr. Brougham* (London, 1830), p. 70.
5. N. Gash, 'The State of the Nation (1822)', in his *Pillars of Government and Other Essays on State and Society, c.1770–c.1880* (London, 1986).
6. Gladstone memorandum, 9 May 1841, printed in J. Brooke and M. Sorenson (eds), *The Prime Ministers' Papers: W. E. Gladstone, II: Autobiographical Memoranda* (London, 1972), pp. 135–37; L. J. Jennings (ed.), *The Correspondence and Diaries of the Late Right Honourable John Wilson Croker* (London, 1885), ii, p. 82.
7. See, for example, E. A. Smith, 'The Yorkshire Electors of 1806 and 1807: A Study on Electoral Management', *Northern History*, 1967.
8. For details of the whips' activities, see A. Aspinall, 'English Party Organisation in the Early Nineteenth Century', *English Historical Review*, July 1926.

9. P. Fraser, 'Party Voting in the House of Commons, 1812–1827', *English Historical Review*, October 1983, p. 773.

10. P. J. V. Rolo, *George Canning: Three Biographical Studies* (London, 1965), p. 3.

11. J. B. Owen, *The Pattern of Politics in Eighteenth-Century England* (London, 1962), p. 3. This short pamphlet is an excellent brief introduction to the subject.

12. A. D. Kriegel, 'Liberty and Whiggery in Early Nineteenth-Century England', *Journal of Modern History*, June 1980, p. 254.

13. See D. E. D. Beales, 'Parliamentary Parties and the "Independent" Member, 1810–1860', in R. Robson (ed.), *Ideas and Institutions of Victorian Britain* (London, 1967); see also O'Gorman, *Two-Party System*, pp. 62–65.

14. A. Mitchell, *The Whigs in Opposition, 1815–1830* (London, 1967), p. 66. Mitchell's book is the best study of the pre-reform Whig Party and is also an excellent discussion of the growth and meaning of party before 1832.

15. J. A. Phillips, 'The Structure of Electoral Politics in Unreformed England', *Journal of British Studies*, Autumn, 1979, p. 84; O'Gorman, *Two-Party System*, p. 75.

16. Mitchell, *Whigs in Opposition*, p. 72.

17. Ibid., p. 43.

18. *Croker Diaries*, i, pp. 367–72.

19. E. Burke, *Letters on a Regicide Peace* (London, 1796), Letter 1.

20. J. A. Phillips, 'Popular Politics in Unreformed England', *Journal of Modern History*, December 1980.

21. L. Radzinowicz, *The History of English Criminal Law and its Administration from 1750* (London, 1948–68), i, p. 528.

22. For an excellent brief survey of this subject see R. J. Morris, *Class and Class Consciousness in the Industrial Revolution, 1780–1850* (London, 1979). Also useful is an earlier essay by A. Briggs, 'The Language of "Class" in Early Nineteenth-Century England', in Briggs and J. Saville (eds), *Essays in Labour History* (London, 1960).

23. E. P. Thompson, *The Making of the English Working Class* (London, 1963). For criticism of Thompson's arguments see R. M. Hartwell, 'The Making of the English Working Class?', *Economic History Review*, December 1965.

24. M. I. Thomis and P. Holt, *Threats of Revolution in Britain, 1789–1848* (London, 1977), makes a persuasive argument against the view that there was a revolutionary possibility in these years.

25. N. Gash, *Aristocracy and People. Britain 1815–1865* (London, 1979), p. 68.

26. Fraser, 'Party Voting', p. 766.

27. J. Mill, *An Essay on Government* (Cambridge, 1937 edition), p. 72. (The essay was first published in 1824.)
28. R. J. White, *Radicalism and its Results, 1760–1837* (London, 1965). A more recent, short discussion of radicalism in this period is to be found in H. T. Dickinson, *British Radicalism and the French Revolution, 1789–1815* (Oxford, 1985).

2. THE GREAT REFORM ACT

1. Grey's government was far from being entirely Whig. The three great secretaryships of state were filled by ex-Canningites (Palmerston at the Foreign Office, Melbourne at the Home Office and Goderich at the War Office) and the ultra-Tory Duke of Richmond was postmaster general. But the government's strength rested on the Whig Party and its Radical allies and throughout this chapter the word 'Whig' is used, for convenience, to describe the government and its parliamentary supporters.
2. See E. J. Hobsbawm and G. Rudé, *Captain Swing* (London, 1969). the Penguin edition of 1973 has a new introduction with the authors' comments on remarks made by critics of the book.
3. The Earl of Northbrook (ed.), *Journals and Correspondence of Francis Thornhill Baring, Lord Northbrook* (London, 1902), i, p. 66.
4. *Annual Register*, 1830, p. 146.
5. Anon., *Parties and Factions in England at the Accession of William IV* (London, 1830), 48.
6. Anon., *The Results of the General Election; or, What Has the Duke of Buckingham Gained by the Dissolution?* (London, 1830).
7. *Parties and Factions*, p. 48.
8. The Duke of Buckingham and Chandos, *Memoirs of the Courts and Cabinets of William IV and Victoria* (London, 1861), i, p. 45.
9. E. J. Stapleton (ed.), *Some Official Correspondence of George Canning* (London, 1887), ii, p. 321.
10. *Hansard*, 3rd Series, i, 37–38.
11. Ibid., vii, 1187.
12. It is worth noting that, despite everyone's knowing that the House of Commons had become the centre of politics, the place both where real business was decided and where ministries were made and unmade – 'nobody cares a damn for the House of Lords', Wellington said in 1818; 'the House of Commons is everything in England and the House of Lords nothing' – nine of the thirteen members of Grey's cabinet sat in the upper house. The other four were Viscount Palmerston, a great landowner with an Irish title

(compatible with a seat in the House of Commons), Viscount Althorp, heir to the large estates of the Earl of Spencer, Sir James Graham, a modest landowner, and Charles Grant.

13. N. Gash, *Politics in the Age of Peel* (London, 1953), p. 11.
14. *Hansard*, New Series, vii, 85.
15. Office of the Times, *History of 'The Times'* (London, 1935–48), i, p. 240.
16. 'It has sometimes occurred to me that we ought to try once more whether, by placing ourselves on the middle ground, condemning the conduct of Hunt and his associates, but strenuously resisting the attempt to attack through them the safeguards of the constitution, we could not rally to our standard all moderate and reasonable men (and a great portion of the property of the country), to whom the people might again be brought to look as their natural leaders and protectors.' (Grey to Henry Brougham, 25 August, 1819. H. Brougham, *The Life and Times of Henry, Lord Brougham* (London, 1871), ii, p. 343.)
17. O'Gorman, *Two-Party System*, p. 86.
18. J. Cannon, *Parliamentary Reform, 1640–1832* (Cambridge, 1973), p. 210.
19. Fraser, 'Party Voting', p. 766.
20. The parliamentary battle, which lasted until the early summer of 1832, may be followed in detail in J. R. M. Butler, *The Passing of the Great Reform Bill* (London, 1914), still the most exciting account, and in M. Brock, *The Great Reform Act* (London, 1973).
21. Cannon, *Parliamentary Reform*, p. 221.
22. Henry, Earl Grey (ed.), *The Correspondence of the Late Earl Grey with H.M. King William IV* (London, 1867), i, pp. 96–97.
23. See W. B. Gwyn, *Democracy and the Cost of Politics in Britain* (London, 1962), pp. 39–48.
24. Professor Gash's discussion of the reform act in the first chapter of his *Politics in the Age of Peel* should not be missed. The quotations that follow are all taken from that chapter.
25. The most important of Moore's articles are 'The Other Face of Reform', *Victorian Studies*, September 1961, and 'Concession or Cure: the Sociological Premises of the First Reform Act', *Historical Journal*, March 1966.
26. See Cannon, *Parliamentary Reform*, pp. 246–50, for a summary of the case against Moore. See also E. P. Hennock, 'The Sociological Premises of the First Reform Act: a Critical Note', *Victorian Studies*, March 1971.
27. *Hansard*, 3rd Series, ii, 1190–1205.

28. T. B. Macaulay, *The Works of Lord Macaulay* (London, 1911), ix, pp. 308–9.

29. E. J. Hobsbawm, *Industry and Empire: an Economic History of Britain since 1750* (London, 1968), p. 55.

30. Thompson, *Making of the English Working Class*, p. 817.

31. See J. Hamburger, *James Mill and the Art of Revolution* (New Haven and London, 1963), and D. J. Rowe (ed.), *London Radicalism, 1830–1843: a Selection from the Papers of Francis Place* (London, 1970).

32. For an excellent discussion of the public context in which the parliamentary battle for the reform bill took place see D. Fraser, 'The Agitation for Parliamentary Reform', in J. T. Ward (ed.), *Popular Movements c.1830–1850* (London, 1970).

33. Readers are recommended to turn to Thomis and Holt, *Threats of Revolution*, pp. 85–99, for a balanced and thorough airing of this question. See also J. Stevenson, *Popular Disturbances in England, 1700–1870* (London, 1979), pp. 218–28, and W. H. Maehl, *The Reform Bill of 1832: Why Not Revolution?* (London, 1967).

3. THE STRUCTURE OF POST-REFORM POLITICS

1. J. E. Thorold Rogers (ed.), *Public Addresses of John Bright, M.P.* (London, 1879), p. 29. Bright made the remark during a speech at Rochdale in 1864.

2. Readers must forgive me for losing this reference.

3. W. Ferguson, 'The Reform Act (Scotland) of 1832: Intention and Effect', *Scottish Historical Review*, xiv (1966), 105. The increase in the Scottish borough electorate would have been even larger were it not that, the country being poorer than England, the £10 qualification added comparatively fewer people to the electoral rolls.

4. C. R. Dod, *Electoral Facts from 1832 to 1853 Impartially Stated* (London, 1853).

5. Gash, *Politics in the Age of Peel*, pp. 438–39.

6. Peel to H. Hobhouse, July 1831. Peel MSS. Add.Mss. 40,402, ff.98–101.

7. See, for example, J. A. Phillips, 'The Many Faces of Reform: the Reform Bill and the Electorate', *Parliamentary History*, I (1982).

8. W. L. Guttsman, *The British Political Elite* (London, 1965), p. 41.

9. Ibid., pp. 38–39.

10. J. Morley, *The Life of Richard Cobden* (London, 1910 edition), p. 517.

11. Gwyn, *Democracy and the Cost of Politics*, p. 95.

12. R. J. Olney, *Lincolnshire Politics, 1832–1885* (Oxford, 1973), p. 32.

13. D. le Marchant, *Memoir of John Charles, Viscount Althorp, Third Earl Spencer* (London, 1876), p. 442.
14. White, *Radicalism and its Results*, p. 8.
15. T. J. Nossiter, 'Elections and Political Behaviour in County Durham and Newcastle, 1832–74', D.Phil. thesis, Oxford University, 1968, p. 416.
16. W. I. Jennings, *Party Politics: II, The Growth of Parties* (Cambridge, 1962), p. 93.
17. Nossiter, 'Elections', p. 25.
18. See D. Fraser, *Urban Politics in Victorian England* (London, 1976), pp. 14–16.
19. Ibid., *passim*.
20. Ibid., pp. 28–29.
21. Ibid., p. 55.
22. These figures are extracted from Fraser, ibid., pp. 125, 137.
23. R. Stewart, *The Foundation of the Conservative Party, 1830–1867* (London, 1978), p. 134. Detailed accounts of Conservative electoral and parliamentary organisation may be found in Chapters 6 and 7 of the foregoing and in N. Gash, 'The Organisation of the Conservative Party, 1832–1846. Part I: The Parliamentary Organisation. Part II: The Electoral Organisation', *Parliamentary History*, I (1982) and II (1983). There are no comparable accounts of Whig/Liberal organisation.
24. Stewart, *Conservative Party*, p. 135.
25. J. H. Whyte, 'Daniel O'Connell and the Repeal Party', *Irish Historical Studies*, September 1959, p. 306.
26. A. D. Kriegel (ed.), *The Holland House Diaries, 1831–1840* (London, 1977), p. 273.
27. Earl of Stanhope and E. Cardwell (eds), *Memoirs of the Right Honourable Sir Robert Peel* (London, 1858), ii, pp. 7–11.
28. F. Raumer, *England in 1835* (London, 1836), iii, p. 316.
29. Ibid., i, pp. 77–78.
30. The best treatment of party development in these years is to be found in D. B. Close, 'The Formation of a Two-Party Alignment in the House of Commons Between 1832 and 1841', *English Historical Review*, April 1969.
31. Bonham to Peel, 25 November 1839. Peel MSS. Add.Mss. 40,427, ff.262–63. Bonham's figure has been shown to be accurate by modern research (or perhaps the matter should be put the other way around). Of the 567 members who sat in the House of Commons between 1837 and 1841 only 7, by Close's analysis of divisions, failed to align themselves firmly with one party or the other (ibid., p. 275).

32. D. Large, 'The Decline of "the Party of the Crown" and the Rise of Parties in the House of Lords, 1783–1837', *English Historical Review*, October 1963, p. 669.
33. *Hansard*, 3rd Series, lxxxvi, 1404.
34. Close, 'Two-Party Alignment', p. 266.
35. Phillips, 'Many Faces of Reform', p. 123.
36. Gash, 'Organisation of the Conservative Party', I, p. 137.

4. THE WHIG DECADE

1. *Hansard*, 3rd Series, lviii, 803–4.
2. Ibid., p. 881. In 1848, when a Whig government was again losing public esteem by its inability to carry certain pieces of legislation, Lord John Russell, the prime minister, defended his government in language similar to Macaulay's. 'There have been in the course of the last thirty years very great changes in the mode of conducting the business of the House. . . . When I first entered parliament it was not usual for government to undertake generally all subjects of legislation . . . since the passing of the Reform Bill it has been thought convenient, on every subject on which an alteration of the law is required, that the government should undertake the responsibility of proposing it to parliament.' Later in the session he returned to the theme. 'I must remind the . . . House that the supposed duty of the members of a government to introduce a great number of measures to parliament and to carry those measures through parliament in a session, is a duty which is new to the government of this country. Let me call the attention of the House to the fact that the Ministers of the Crown are chiefly appointed to administer the affairs of the Empire.' (Quoted in H. Parris, *Constitutional Bureaucracy. The Development of British Central Administration Since the Eighteenth Century* (London, 1969) p. 168.)
3. N. Gash, 'The Historical Significance of the Tamworth Manifesto', in *Pillars of Government*, is so thorough and perceptive an analysis that it must be considered the last word on the subject.
4. The prevailing view among historians that the early factory acts (1833, 1844 and 1847) were never adequately enforced because the inspectors were thwarted in their prosecutions of delinquent mill-owners by the leniency of the courts has been effectively challenged by A. E. Peacock, 'The Successful Prosecution of the Factory Acts, 1833–55', *Economic History Review*, May 1984. He has

shown that in nineteen of the twenty-one years under his review the conviction rate was above 80 per cent and in twelve of those years above 90 per cent.

5. On Brougham as a law reformer see R. Stewart, *Henry Brougham, 1778–1868. His Public Career* (London, 1968), pp. 233–38 and 277–85, and D. B. Swinfen, 'Henry Brougham and the Judicial Committee of the Privy Council', *Law Quarterly Review*, July 1974.

6. G. M. Young, *Victorian England. Portrait of an Age*, Oxford, 1960 paperback edition, 44. Mr Young's classic essay, first published in 1936, allusive and sometimes whimsical, remains the most beguiling watercolour treatment of the Victorian age. 'For that matter, what is History about?' he asked in the introduction to the 1953 edition. 'And the conclusion I reached was that the real, central theme of History is not what happened, but what people felt about it when it was happening.'

7. E. Halévy, *The Triumph of Reform (1830–1841)* (London, 1961 edition), p. 130.

8. *Times*, 26 February 1836.

9. *Hansard*, 3rd Series, xxiii, 666.

10. J. Prest, *Lord John Russell* (London, 1972), p. 65.

11. See A. D. Kriegel, 'The Politics of the Whigs in Opposition, 1834–1835', *Journal of British Studies*, May 1968.

12. See I. D. C. Newbould, 'Whiggery and the Dilemma of Reform: Liberals, Radicals and the Melbourne Administration, 1835–9', *Bulletin of the Institute of Historical Research*, November 1980.

13. This was the accusation brought against the clergy by the Reform Association (Close, 'Two-Party Alignment', p. 267).

14. Peel to J. Croker, 12 November 1837. *Croker Diaries*, ii, pp. 320–21.

15. N. Gash, *Reaction and Reconstruction in English Politics, 1832–1852* (Oxford, 1965), 69n.

16. G. Kitson Clark, *Peel and the Conservative Party* (London, 1929), p. 409.

17. See M. A. G. O. Tuathaigh, 'The Irish in Nineteenth-Century Britain: Problems of Integration', *Transactions of the Royal Historical Society*, 1981.

18. *Times*, 21 June 1837.

19. Young, *Victorian England*, p. 30.

20. Croker to Peel, 20 July 1841. C. S. Parker, *Sir Robert Peel from his Private Papers* (London, 1899), ii, p. 475.

21. N. Gash, 'Wellington and Peel, 1832–1846', in D. Southgate (ed.), *The Conservative Leadership, 1832–1932* (London, 1974), pp. 46–47.

22. See the tables in Fraser, *Urban Politics*, 227, and Stewart, *Conserva-*

tive Party, 384–5; and, more generally, Stewart, pp. 151–65 and I. D. C. Newbould, 'Sir Robert Peel and the Conservative Party, 1832–41: A Study in Failure?', *English Historical Review*, July 1983.

5. PEEL AND THE NEW CONSERVATISM

1. These figures are taken from the analysis of the election returns made by the chief whip, Thomas Fremantle (Fremantle MSS, 110/9). The Conservatives made a net gain of 23 seats in the English and Welsh counties and 8 seats in the English and Welsh boroughs. Fremantle gave the Conservatives a majority of 76; on the vote in the new parliament which raised them to office they had a majority of 91.

2. See Hobsbawm, *Industry and Empire*, pp. 57–58.

3. Ripon to Graham, July 1841. Peel MSS. Add.Mss. 40,446, f.5.

4. *Hansard*, 3rd Series, lix, 555.

5. N. Gash, *Sir Robert Peel. The Life of Sir Robert Peel after 1830* (London, 1972), p. 360.

6. *Maidstone Journal*, 12 April 1842.

7. Parker, *Peel*, ii, p. 551.

8. Prest, *Russell*, pp. 189–90.

9. See G. L. Mosse, 'The Anti-League: 1844–1846', *Economic History Review*, December 1947, and M. Lawson-Tancred, 'The Anti-League and the Corn Law Crisis of 1846', *Historical Journal*, June 1960.

10. Gash, *Sir Robert Peel*, pp. 439–40.

11. Bonham to Peel [June 1844]. Peel MSS. Add.Mss. 40,547, ff.1–2.

12. For somewhat differing views of the importance of the 1844 revolts for the state of the Conservative Party see R. Stewart, 'The Ten Hours and Sugar Crises of 1844: Government and the House of Commons in the Age of Reform', *Historical Journal*, March 1969, and D. R. Fisher, 'Peel and the Conservative Party: The Sugar Crisis of 1844 Reconsidered', ibid., June 1975.

13. J. B. Conacher, *The Peelites and the Party System* (Newton Abbot, 1972), p. 11.

14. R. Vyvyan, *A Letter from Sir Richard Vyvyan, Bart., M.P., to his Constituents upon the Commercial and Financial Policy of Sir Robert Peel's Administration* (London, 1842), p. 32.

15. Peel to Lady de Grey, 21 June 1844. Peel MSS. Add.Mss. 40,547, ff.136–39.

16. Gash, *Reaction and Reconstruction*, p. 130.

17. Pusey to the Duke of Richmond, 10 April 1842. Goodwood MSS,

Box 41/75. Richmond emerged in the next couple of years as a leader of the protectionist Anti-League.

18. For the Conservative government's handling of Irish ecclesiastical and religious issues see D. A. Kerr, *Peel, Priests and Politics* (Oxford, 1982).

19. An excellent summary of the Maynooth episode is to be found in E. R. Norman, *Anti-Catholicism in Victorian England* (London, 1968), pp. 23–51. The college had been founded in 1795 on a grant of money voted by the old Dublin parliament and the grant was transferred to the imperial parliament at the Union of Ireland and Great Britain in 1801 as a concession to Irish Roman Catholics. Pitt preferred to support the training of priests in Ireland than to see novices travel to French seminaries, where they might be infected with revolutionary and anti-English political doctrines.

20. T. E. Kebbel, *History of Toryism from 1783 to 1881* (London, 1886), p. 289.

21. *Hansard*, 3rd Series, lxxvii, 78.

22. See D. M. Thompson, 'The Liberation Society, 1844–1868', in P. Hollis (ed.), *Pressure from Without in Early Victorian England* (London, 1974).

23. See G. A. Cahill, 'The Protestant Association and the anti-Maynooth Agitation of 1845', *Catholic Historical Review*, October 1957, and G. I. T. Machin, 'The Maynooth Grant, the Dissenters and Disestablishment, 1845–47', *English Historical Review*, January 1967.

24. Gladstone memorandum, 14 January 1845. Gladstone MSS. Add.Mss. 44,777, ff.212–15.

25. Diary, 7th Earl of Shaftesbury, 19 March 1845. Broadlands MSS, SHA/PD/3.

26. Graham to H. Hardinge, 23 April 1845 (copy). Graham MSS (microfilm), 148/23.

27. *Hansard*, 3rd Series, lxxix, 565–69.

6. FREE TRADE AND ITS AFTERMATH

1. See B. Hilton, 'Peel: A Reappraisal', *Historical Journal*, September 1979, which argues against the orthodox view of Peel as a 'statesman' whose mind was moved slowly by 'facts' towards a free-trade position in favour of the view that on financial matters facts were rarely allowed to interfere with reasoning from abstract principles in Peel's mind.

2. See S. Fairlie, 'The Corn Laws and British Wheat Production, 1829–1876', *Economic History Review*, April 1969.

3. Gash, *Aristocracy and People*, p. 237.

4. Peel to E. B. Denison, 7 January 1846. Peel MSS. Add.Mss. 40,532, ff.89–90.

5. Parker, *Peel*, ii, p. 529.

6. *Hansard*, 3rd Series, lviii, 1240.

7. Ibid., lxxxiii, 95.

8. The phrases quoted are from the *Quarterly Review*, June 1847. The *Quarterly*, which was the leading Conservative review from its foundation in 1809, remained sympathetic to protection in 1846 and afterwards.

9. *Croker Diaries*, iii, p. 68.

10. The phrase, used much later, was Disaraeli's. John Prest makes the nice remark that 'the chalice was already poisoned when Lord John passed it over in 1841' (Prest, *Russell*, p. 188). For the Whigs' failure to take office in 1845 see F. A. Dreyer, 'The Whigs and the Political Crisis of 1845', *English Historical Review*, July 1965.

11. Quoted in W. Johnston, *England As It Is, Political, Social, and Industrial, in the Middle of the Nineteenth Century* (London, 1851), i, p. 20.

12. A. Alison, *The Principles of Population and Their Connection with Human Happiness* (Edinburgh, 1840), i, p. 50.

13. Raumer, *England in 1835*, ii, pp. 172–73.

14. There have been many biographies of Cobden since John Morley published the first of real worth in 1881. Nicholas Edsall's recent study, *Richard Cobden: Independent Radical* (Cambridge, Massachusetts, 1987), is the only one to emphasise the possibility that Cobden's antipathy towards the gentry may owe more to his rural upbringing than his Manchester experience.

15. Morley, *Cobden*, i, pp. 140–41.

16. *Croker Diaries*, iii, p. 13.

17. See R. Stewart, *The Politics of Protection. Lord Derby and the Protectionist Party* (London, 1971), p. 36.

18. For the organisation and activities of the Anti-League see Stewart, *Conservative Party*, pp. 206–12.

19. Diary, 7th Earl of Shaftesbury, 9 and 12 February 1846. Broadlands MSS, SHA/PD/4.

20. Lord George Bentinck to the Duke of Portland, 11 and 13 February 1846. Portland MSS, PWH/203, 205.

21. See N. Gash, 'Lord George Bentinck and his Sporting World', in *Pillars of Government*, for a discussion of why it was that Bentinck's political opponents believed him to have 'imported into the arts

of parliamentary leadership a new and degrading element'. Bentinck led the Protectionist Party in the House of Commons from 1846 to 1848; for those two years he was as much a stumbling block in the way of Conservative reunion as Disraeli was.

22. *Hansard*, 3rd Series, lxxxiii, 122–23.
23. Parker, *Peel*, iii, p. 364.
24. J. K. Glynn, 'The Private Member of Parliament, 1833–1868', Ph.D. thesis, University of London, 1949, pp. 37, 40.
25. *Phineas Redux*, Chapter 40. The 'conjurer' was Disraeli, represented in the novel by the Conservative leader, Mr Daubeny.
26. W. O. Aydelotte, 'The Country Gentlemen and the Repeal of the Corn Laws', *English Historical Review*, January 1967, p. 54.
27. Johnston, *England As It Is*, i, p. 193.
28. *Hansard*, 3rd Series, lxxxvii, 1054–55.
29. For the Protectionists see Stewart, *Politics of Protection*, and for the Peelites, Conacher, *Peelites and the Party System*.
30. Hobsbawm, *Industry and Empire*, p. 86.

7. REFORM AND THE DISPOSSESSED

1. T. J. Nossiter, 'Aspects of Electoral Behaviour in English Constituencies, 1832–1868', in E. Allard and S. Rokkan (eds), *Mass Politics* (New York, 1970), p. 167.
2. For a brief account of Tory Radicalism and the formation of these societies see Stewart, *Conservative Party*, pp. 165–71.
3. T. C. Smout, *A Century of the Scottish People, 1830–1950* (London, 1986), p. 15.
4. Hobsbawm, *Industry and Empire*, p. 55.
5. Quoted in W. E. Houghton, *The Victorian Frame of Mind, 1830–1870* (New Haven and London, 1957), p. 29.
6. J. H. Buckley, *The Victorian Temper. A Study in Literary Culture* (Cambridge, Massachusetts, 1951), p. 119. Buckley takes from Henry Porter's contemporary *Progress of the Nation* the quite startling, and no doubt quite exceptional, figures of the reading material available at one London teashop: 43 London daily newspapers, seven provincial newspapers, six foreign newspapers, 24 monthly magazines, four quarterly reviews and eleven weeklies.
7. Smout, *Scottish People*, pp. 141–46.
8. R. K. Webb, *The British Working Class Reader, 1790–1848* (London, 1955), p. 33.
9. Quoted in A. Briggs, *The Age of Improvement, 1783–1867* (London, 1959), p. 290.

10. A guide to the literature on this vexed question may be found in R. M. Hartwell, 'The Rising Standard of Living in England, 1800–1850' and 'The Standard of Living: an Answer to the Pessimists', in his *The Industrial Revolution and Economic Growth* (London, 1971).

11. 'The Budget and the Reform Bill', *Quarterly Review*, April 1860.

12. Johnston, *England As It Is*, i, p. 82.

13. See M. Blaug, 'The Myth of the Old Poor Law and the Making of the New', *Journal of Economic History*, XXIII, 1963, and D. A. Baugh, 'The Cost of Poor Relief in South-East England, 1790–1834', *Economic History Review*, February 1975.

14. Brougham, *Life and Times*, iii, pp. 322–23.

15. See P. Dunkley, 'Whigs and Paupers: The Reform of the English Poor Laws, 1830–1834', *Journal of British Studies*, Spring, 1981.

16. The best treatment of this campaign is N. C. Edsall, *The anti-Poor Law Movement, 1834–44* (Manchester, 1971). A more recent account, J. Knott, *Popular Opposition to the 1834 Poor Law* (London, 1986), is less satisfactory. For a brief resumé of the subject see M. E. Rose, 'The Anti-Poor Law Agitation', in Ward, *Popular Movements*.

17. Halévy, *Triumph of Reform*, p. 323.

18. The literature on Chartism is vast. A brief, though now somewhat dated, survey of it is to be found in A. Wilson, 'Chartism', in Ward, *Popular Movements*. The best general treatment is D. Thompson, *The Chartists. Popular Politics in the Industrial Revolution* (London, 1984). Still valuable are G. D. H. Cole, *Chartist Portraits* (London, 1941), and A. Briggs (ed.), *Chartist Studies* (London, 1959).

19. White, *Radicalism and its Results*, p. 11.

20. The transformation of the moral climate of upper-class and middle-class English society between the late-18th century and the accession of Queen Victoria is the subject of the delightful book by M. Jaeger, *Before Victoria: Changing Standards and Behaviour, 1787–1837* (London, 1956).

21. There is a large body of literature on early Victorian social legislation. Two thorough and balanced accounts are D. Roberts, *Victorian Origins of the British Welfare State* (New Haven, 1968), and W. C. Lubenow, *The Politics of Government Growth* (Newton Abbot, 1971). An excellent essay on the 'revolution in government' of the 1830s and 1840s is A. J. Taylor, *Laissez-faire and State Intervention in Nineteenth-century Britain* (London, 1972).

22. D. Marshall, *Industrial England, 1776–1851* (London, 1973), p. 196.

23. Quoted by P. Pulzer, *London Review of Books*, 4 September 1986.

24. Thomis and Holt, *Threats of Revolution*, p. 127.

25. Stevenson, *Popular Disturbances*, p. 320.
26. M. Sadleir, *Trollope. A Commentary* (London, 1945 edition), pp. 145–46.

SELECT BIBLIOGRAPHY

This highly selective list of books and articles is meant simply to serve as a guide to further reading for students and undergraduates.

BOOKS

Adelman, P., *Victorian Radicalism. The Middle-Class Experience, 1830–1914,* (London, 1984).

Briggs, A. (ed.), *Chartist Studies* (London, 1965).

Brock, M., *The Great Reform Act* (London, 1973).

Cannon, J., *Parliamentary Reform, 1640–1832* (Cambridge, 1973).

Checkland, S. G., *The Rise of Industrial Society in England, 1815–1885* (London, 1964).

Conacher, J. B., *The Peelites and the Party System* (Newton Abbot, 1972).

Davis, R. W., Political Change and Continuity, 1760–1885. *A Buckinghamshire Study* (Newton Abbot, 1972).

Dickinson, H. T., *British Radicalism and the French Revolution, 1789–1815,* (Oxford, 1985).

Edsall, N. C., *The anti-Poor Law Movement, 1834–44* (Manchester, 1971).

Epstein, J., and Thompson, D. (eds), *The Chartist Experience: Studies in Working-Class Radicalism and Culture, 1830–60* (London, 1982).

Foster, J., *Class Struggle and the Industrial Revolution. Early Industrial Capitalism in Three English Towns* (London, 1974).

Fraser, D., *Urban Politics in Victorian England* (London, 1976).

Gash, N., *Aristocracy and People. Britain 1815–1865* (London, 1979).

——, *Politics in the Age of Peel* (London, 1953).

——, *Reaction and Reconstruction in English Politics, 1832–1852* (Oxford, 1965).

Hartwell, R. M., *The Industrial Revolution and Economic Growth* (London, 1971).

Hill, B. W., *British Parliamentary Parties, 1742–1832* (London, 1985).

Hobsbawm, E. J., *Industry and Empire: an Economic History of Britain since 1750* (London, 1968).

Hobsbawm, E. J., and Rudé, G., *Captain Swing* (London, 1973 edition).

Hollis, P. (ed.), *Pressure from Without in Early Victorian England* (London, 1974).

Kitson Clark, G., *The Making of Victorian England* (London, 1962).

——, *An Expanding Society. Britain 1830–1900* (Cambridge, 1967).

Lubenow, W. C., *The Politics of Government Growth* (Newton Abbot, 1971).

Marshall, D., *Industrial England, 1776–1851* (London, 1973).

Mitchell, A., *The Whigs in Opposition, 1815–1830* (London, 1967).

Morris, R. J., *Class and Class Consciousness in the Industrial Revolution, 1780–1850* (London, 1979).

Neale, R. S., *Class and Ideology in the Nineteenth Century* (London, 1972).

O'Gorman, F., *The Emergence of the British Two-Party System, 1760–1832* (London, 1982).

Perkin, H., *The Origins of Modern English Society, 1780–1880* (London, 1969).

Raumer, F., *England in 1835* (London, 1836).

Roberts, D., *Victorian Origins of the British Welfare State* (New Haven, 1968).

Southgate, D., *The Passing of the Whigs, 1832–1886* (London, 1962).

Stevenson, J., *Popular Disturbances in England, 1700–1870* (London, 1979).

Stewart, R., *The Politics of Protection. Lord Derby and the Protectionist Party, 1841–1852* (Cambridge, 1971).

——, *The Foundation of the Conservative Party, 1830–1867* (London, 1978).

Taylor, A. J., *Laissez-faire and State Intervention in Nineteenth-century Britain* (London, 1972).

Thomis, M. I., and Holt, P., *Threats of Revolution in Britain, 1789–1848* (London, 1977).

Thompson, D., *The Chartists. Popular Politics in the Industrial Revolution* (London, 1984).

Thompson, F. M. L., *English Landed Society in the Nineteenth Century* (London, 1963).

Vincent, J., *Pollbooks. How Victorians Voted* (Cambridge, 1968).

Ward, J. T. (ed.), *Popular Movements c.1830–1850* (London, 1970).

ARTICLES

Aydelotte, W. O., 'The Country Gentlemen and the Repeal of the Corn Laws', *English Historical Review*, January, 1967.

Baugh, D. A., 'The Cost of Poor Relief in South-east England, 1790–1834', *Economic History Review*, February, 1975.

Beales, D. E. D., 'Parliamentary Parties and the "Independent" Member, 1810–1860', in R. Robson (ed.), *Ideas and Institutions of Victorian Britain* (London, 1967).

——, 'Peel, Russell and Reform', *Historical Journal*, December, 1974.

Cahill, G. A., 'Irish Catholicism and English Toryism', *Review of Politics*, January, 1957.

Close, D. H., 'The Formation of a Two-Party Alignment in the House of Commons Between 1832 and 1841', *English Historical Review*, April, 1969.

Condon, M. D., 'The Irish Church and the Reform Ministries', *Journal of British Studies*, May, 1964.

Davis, R. W., 'The Whigs and the Idea of Electoral Reform: Some Further Thoughts on the Great Reform Act', *Durham University Journal*, December, 1974.

Dreyer, F. A., 'The Whigs and the Political Crisis of 1845', *English Historical Review*, July, 1965.

Dunkley, P., 'Whigs and Paupers: the Reform of the English Poor Laws, 1830–1834', *Journal of British Studies*, Spring, 1981.

Fairlie, S., 'The Nineteenth-Century Corn Law Reconsidered', *Economic History Review*, December, 1965.

——, 'The Corn Laws and British Wheat Production, 1829–76', *Economic History Review*, April, 1969.

Fraser, P., 'Party Voting in the House of Commons, 1812–1827', *English Historical Review*, October, 1983.

Gash, N., 'Peel and the Party System, 1830–50', *Transactions of the Royal Historical Society*, 5th Series, 1950.

——, 'The Organisation of the Conservative Party, 1832–1846. Part I: The Parliamentary Organisation. Part II: The Electoral Organisation', *Parliamentary History*, I (1982) and II (1983).

Gross, I., 'The Abolition of Negro Slavery and British Parliamentary Politics, 1832–3', *Historical Journal*, March, 1980.

Gunn, J. A. W., 'Influence, Parties and the Constitution: Changing Attitudes, 1783–1832', *Historical Journal*, June, 1974.

Heesom, A., 'The Coal Mines Act of 1842, Social Reform, and Social Control', *Historical Journal*, March, 1981

Hennock, E. P., 'The Sociological Premises of the First Reform Act: a Critical Note', *Victorian Studies*, March, 1971.

Hilton, B., 'Peel: a Reappraisal', *Historical Journal*, September, 1979.

Kitson Clark, G., 'The Electorate and the Repeal of the Corn Laws', *Transactions of the Royal Historical Society*, 5th Series, 1951.

Kriegel, A. D., 'The Politics of the Whigs in Opposition, 1834–1835', *Journal of British Studies*, May, 1968.

——, 'Liberty and Whiggery in Early Nineteenth Century England', *Journal of Modern History*, June, 1980.

Large, D., 'The Decline of the "Party of the Crown" and the Rise of Parties in the House of Lords, 1783–1837', *English Historical Review*, October, 1963.

Lawson-Tancred, M., 'The Anti-League and the Corn Law Crisis of 1846', *Historical Journal*, June, 1960.

Machin, G. I. T., 'The Maynooth Grant, the Dissenters and Disestablishment, 1845–47', *English Historical Review*, January, 1967.

Moore, D. C., 'The Other Face of Reform', *Victorian Studies*, September, 1961.

——, 'Concession or Cure: the Sociological Premises of the First Reform Act', *Historical Journal*, March, 1966.

——, 'The Corn Laws and High Farming', *Economic History Review*, December, 1965.

Mosse, G. L., 'The Anti-League: 1844–46', *Economic History Review*, December, 1947.

Newbould, I. D. C., 'Whiggery and the Dilemma of Reform: Liberals, Radicals and the Melbourne Administration, 1835–9', *Bulletin of the Institute of Historical Research*, November, 1980.

——, 'Sir Robert Peel and the Conservative Party, 1832–1841: A Study in Failure?', *English Historical Review*, July, 1983.

O'Neill, M., and Martin, G., 'A Backbencher on Parliamentary Reform, 1831–1832', *Historical Journal*, September, 1980.

Ó Tuathaigh, M. A. G., 'The Irish in Nineteenth-Century Britain: Problems of Integration', *Transactions of the Royal Historical Society*, 5th Series, 1981.

Phillips, J. A., 'The Structure of Electoral Politics in Unreformed England', *Journal of British Studies*, Autumn, 1979.

——, 'Popular Politics in Unreformed England', *Journal of Modern History*, December, 1980.

——, 'The Many Faces of Reform: the Reform Bill and the Electorate', *Parliamentary History*, I (1982).

Spring, D., 'The English Landed Estate in the Age of Coal and Iron: 1830–1880', *Journal of Economic History*, Winter, 1951.

Stewart, R., 'The Ten Hours and Sugar Crises of 1844: Government and the House of Commons in the Age of Reform', *Historical Journal*, March, 1969.

Strachan, H., 'The Early Victorian Army and the Nineteenth-Century Revolution in Government', *English Historical Review*, October, 1980.

INDEX